Healing
with
Gemstones
and
Crystals

by Diane Stein

THE CROSSING PRESS
FREEDOM, CALIFORNIA

For Brede

—————————※—————————

Copyright © 1996 by Diane Stein
Cover and interior design by Tara M. Eoff
Cover photo courtesy of Digital Stock Corp.
Back cover photo by Davida Johns.
Printed in U.S.A.

For information on bulk purchases or group discounts for this and other
Crossing Press titles, please contact our Special Sales Manager at
800-777-1048.

Healing and medicine are two very different disciplines and the law
requires the following disclaimer. The information in this book is not
medicine but healing, and it does not constitute medical advice. In case of
serious illness consult the practitioner of your choice.

Library of Congress Cataloging-in-Publication Data

Stein, Diane, 1948-
Healing with Gemstones and Crystals / by Diane Stein.
      p.   cm.
      Includes bibliographical references (p.).
      ISBN 0-89594-831-1
      1. Precious stones-Miscellanea. 2. Crystals--Psychic aspects.
3. Healing 4. Occultism I. Title.
BF1442.P74S75 1996
133--dc20   96-9033
                                                          CIP

I would like to thank the following people for their help with this book. First, I thank Jim and Sandy from The Crystal Connection, Indian Rocks Beach, Florida, and Joy Weaver of Treasures Bookstore in Tampa. These loving people allowed me to go through their amazing stock of crystals and gemstones and to sit on their floor to channel definitions for them, despite hectic business and the Christmas rush. I also thank Karen Silverman and Corinne Nichols, who encouraged the whole project and brought me their own gemstones to add to the catalog and Dorothy Byrne, who is wonderful at calming me down when I am under stress. Dorothy said she never felt anything from crystals—until I put a piece of Zincite into her hand.

Thanks also to Elaine Gill of The Crossing Press, who decided it was finally time to put my gemstone mania into print, and Victoria, Amy, Karen, Cyndi; and the production team who turn my scribbles into wonderful books. Special and heartfelt thanks goes to Brigid Fuller, who publicizes my books so well and supports the processes throughout.

This book could not have been written without the discarnate help of Brede (Bride, Bridgit), who lovingly channeled it through me. May The Maiden's blessings reach all who read and use it.

Contents

Introduction

❖

Gemstones and crystals are magickal, in the true meaning of magick which is defined as being part of the natural wonders of the Earth. Gemstones and crystals are part of the Earth Herself since fully a third of the composition of our Goddess planet is made of quartz, and the silica and water that crystal is composed of are also major components of our physical bodies. Quartz is fossilized water and our bodies are 98 percent water. The Earth's magnetic field is crystal and gemstone vibrational energy and so is the magnetic field of the human aura. Crystals' piezoelectric effects, their energy fields, and the energy fields of other gemstones match our human energy and electrical frequencies. Because they do, they can be used as tools for energy rebalancing when human frequencies need alignment or healing. We are all a part of Goddess Earth and so are the gemstones and crystals found within Her.

A network of crystal and gemstone energy intersects the Earth. At ground level this network is formed of the ley lines, the planet's acupuncture map. Beyond Earth's body and mirrored in the human mental body aura is the universal grid. This is formed by crystal and gemstone energy radiating from the planet and the galaxy and also is incorporated into human energy. The Wiccan adage for this is, "As above, so below." The grid contains our individual minds and the Collective Mind of society, as well as access to the Universal Mind of Goddess, or the all-creative Void. The grid is the interface between our auras and that of the Earth and universe. The crystal grid is also the energy transmitter of the Nonvoid, the Goddess within way in which mind creates matter from the Goddess Void. It is our human connection between Goddess and the individual, and between the individual and the Stars.

Connecting Earth's ley lines to Her mental aura energy grid is a series of giant tuning crystals, some of them not clear quartz but other gemstones. They are mostly underground or underwater. These physically exist on the planet, scattered around the globe in key places. Many of them are sites sacred to local peoples who still practice ancient ways. Some of them are unknown or forgotten. These crystals have been dormant or nearly so for thousands of years. They were deactivated at the time that human DNA was willfully unplugged in a war between other-planetary forces over control of the developing Earth. The result was the reducing of human information and energy from a twelve-paired double helix to our current two-stranded one.[1] That time was not so long ago, probably occurring in the same period that the Goddess was dethroned by the male patriarchal order. The deactivated crystal grid was a major part of the information network that is our human heritage.

Human energy and Earth's crystal grid, as well as all the crystals and gemstones of the planet, are now waking up. The crystal grid is reactivating and slowly clearing. As each giant of the grid opens, clears, and heals, it in turn reopens, clears, and heals the next smaller stones around it. As the next stones awaken, they too awaken those that are the next smaller. The ultimate goal is to awaken, clear, and heal all the crystals and gemstones of the Earth, from the energy grid giants down to the tiny ones in computer chips and jewelry. By healing all the crystals, the energy frequency of the planet is being healed. In healing Earth's planetary crystal energy, all human energy is also being reactivated, tuned, and expanded. Human DNA will be healed and reconnected as the process slowly proceeds over the next several decades.

Crystals and gemstones have always been used by healers. Because of their current energy activation they are now becoming an even more primary factor for healing people and the Goddess Earth. As the crystals and gemstones are opening and healing, their expanded frequencies also heal people by opening, tuning, and programming human auras. The giant stones are a connecting link between the ley line system and the universal mind grid. The stones' activation connects the human aura to the universal grid as well as to our own Bodies of Light. This energy body is the core soul level of the mental body that remains aware through the soul's many lifetimes and between lifetimes. People are intrinsic in the universal Goddess plan, our minds and Light Bodies are part of the universal Goddess Mind. Because of the stones' activation, galactic and solar system energy can now reach us through the grid. We are also being helped by advanced positive healers from other planets.

The little crystals and colored gemstones in our pockets and jewelry do more for us than we know, and their energy is increasing in usefulness as time goes on. As Goddess Earth awakens and heals, so the crystals and gemstones, her healing tools, awaken all Earth's people, animals, every living thing. We are becoming much more than people can ever remember being before; we are becoming the Be-ings of Light, energy, and information, that was our original heritage. Human twelve-strand DNA contains the genetic keys of all life in the universe, what Barbara Marciniak in her book *Earth* calls the Living Library.[2] That library is being repaired, healed, reactivated, and returned to us primarily by way of gemstones and crystals.

1 For further information on this, read Barbara Marciniak, *Earth: Pleiadian Keys to the Living Library* (Santa Fe, N.M.: Bear & Co., 1995), 12–16; and *Bringers of the Dawn: Teachings from the Pleiadians* (Santa Fe, N.M.: Bear & Co., 1992), 13–19.
2 Barbara Marciniak, *Earth: Pleiadian Keys to the Living Library*, 12–16.

How to Choose Gemstones

People today are increasingly drawn to gemstones and crystals, to wearing them as jewelry, keeping them on display in their homes, and using them consciously on every level for healing and energy work. Often, those who work with stones have no cosmic understanding about them; they only know that they want the beauty of crystals and gemstones around them in their homes and in their lives. Whether chosen deliberately for specific healing purposes or not, the "right" gem energies reach the people who choose them. When women ask me which stone to buy or in what form, I tell them simply, "Take the one(s) you are the most drawn to." That particular gemstone or type of stone invariably will be what you need at the present time.

Gemstones and crystals come in many forms, and as long as the stone is natural rather than humanmade, all the forms are positive for healing. Some people prefer rough gemstone specimens right from the Earth, while others like the stones polished, cut, and faceted. Some prefer using smooth, tumbled stones, gemstone eggs, or stones shaped into wands, spheres, or carvings. Rough stones in matrix may be less expensive than those that are cut and faceted by jewelers. Tumbled stones are usually inexpensive, and gemstone spheres and eggs are coming down in price. Gemstone jewelry is becoming more and more available in a wide price range. Gemstone specimens come in all sizes and all grades. Pick the size that is comfortable for your chosen use and the grade that is attractive in its price and aesthetics. Stones with clearer colors have stronger energy, as do stones that are larger in size, but all natural stones have healing energy and there are many choices.

Stones can be used in a room for decoration while healing the environmental energy. They can be placed under a bed, massage table, or healing table, or on a Goddess or meditation altar. Usually, larger stones are used for these purposes. Smaller gemstones and crystals can be carried in your pockets or held in your hand while sleeping. After a few nights' practice they will stay in place. They can be used in necklaces, rings, pins, earrings, or bracelets, as single stones or combinations of them. In healing, they can be draped over the chakras or they can be taped to the skin.

An ancient use for Quartz Crystal and some gemstones (Clear Beryl, Obsidian, and Smoky Quartz particularly) was scrying—looking into the stone for divination and prophecy—and using the gem as a focusing tool for meditation and channeling. Gemstones can also be made into elixirs and used as pendulums. The key to using stones for healing is simply to place them into your aura (your body's energy field), on or very near your body. The stone can be anything that appeals to you.

Pick up the gemstone or crystal that most attracts you and hold it in your left hand. The left side of the body brings energy/information in more strongly than the right side for most people, whether they are right- or left-handed. Close your eyes, still your mind, and focus on the stone. Notice what you sense and feel, both from the stone and in yourself. Become aware of the energy of the stone, giving yourself some time to do this. If you perceive no sensation after several quiet minutes, try switching hands, or try a different crystal or gemstone in your left hand. Notice your mood and if there has been a change in it. If you are new to crystal work, learning to sense energy may take some practice. Gemstone and crystal energy is delicate and subtle, and the sensations will be delicate and subtle as well. Whether you perceive the energy of the stone or not, it will still affect you.

You may feel a tingling sensation, you may be aware of bright lights or colors (not necessarily the color of the stone), you may feel vibration, energy waves, magnetic sensations, heat, or cold. You may be given an image, like running water or a place on or within the Earth. You may be able or unable to identify the source. There may be sounds of bells, rain, or music. You may see a past lifetime or someone you love, or be given information in words or impressions. Your mood may lighten or become calmer or more excited. No two people will experience gemstone energy or the energy of a particular gemstone or crystal in the same way. Any or all of the senses may be involved: the impressions may not be visual. The sensations are a part of your own energy vibration in combination with that of the gemstone. If the sensations delight or interest you and feel good to you—if they give you something you need—the stone is positive for your use in healing and is a good choice.

Clearing Gemstones and Crystals

Sometimes a stone you are strongly drawn to doesn't feel good, or a stone that felt good previously doesn't feel good now. The stone or crystal may be in need of clearing. To clear a gemstone or crystal means cleansing it of extraneous energy from others or yourself that it may be holding. Stones absorb energy from anyone who handles them, and quartz crystals and many gemstones heal pain by taking it into themselves. If these unwanted energies are left in the stone, it will eventually clear itself, but in the meantime its ability as a healing tool will be greatly decreased. Very overloaded stones sometimes self-destruct, shatter, fall, or get lost, and an uncleared pendulum will lose all accuracy. Uncleared stones can transmit another person's pain to the next person who holds the stone. The clearer the energy of a healing stone, the more useful it is.

Gemstone users sometimes keep other people from touching their stones. I do not feel this to be necessary. If a person is someone whose energy you want in your life, they cannot harm you or your crystals by touching them. Gemstones are healing tools, and if a person is in pain—whether the stone's owner or someone else—the stone will help them. Stones used for healing or in laying on of stones are used intentionally to absorb others' pain. So are gemstones or crystals worn as jewelry, kept in a room, or used in any other way. Any pain or negative energy a stone absorbs can be easily cleared, and most of the pain held in a stone is from its owner-user.

Crystals and healing gemstones need clearing as soon as they are purchased. They also need clearing after every use in healing; if they are used during a massage; after gemstone jewelry is worn; after a stone is carried in your pocket; or after you have slept with a gemstone under your pillow. Pendulums may be accurate for only a few hours if they are heavily used; they need frequent clearing. Gemstones and crystals used on altars and as room energy healers need clearing regularly as well, more often in times of sickness or emotional distress than at other times. Daily is not too often to clear actively used stones, and weekly clearing may be necessary for those used in the environment. When I lay on stones, I prefer to clear them before and after each healing.

There are any number of effective ways to clear crystals and gemstones. If nothing else is available, simply run them under cold tap water. (This is not as effective as other methods.) Always use cold water, as crystals can shatter when exposed to heat, and allow them to remain in the flowing water for several minutes. Where stones have pointed terminations, as clear crystals do, point them toward the drain as the water runs on them. Do not clear Halite specimens in running water—the mineral (salt crystal) will dissolve.

Salt, in fact, is the most accepted and probably the most powerful method for clearing crystals. I recommend it for the initial cleansing of a new healing stone and for any time a stone is overloaded with negative energy or pain. You may wish to try methods other than salt, which strips everything except the programming (see next section) from a stone. Salt can be dissolved in water or used dry. To use salt water, mix a tablespoonful of sea salt in a glass or ceramic cup of cold water. Do not use plastic or metal containers. Place the stones to be cleared in the solution and allow them to soak for several hours or overnight. Highly overloaded stones may need to soak longer. To use dry salt, place dry sea salt in a glass or non-plastic container and bury the stones to be cleared in the salt. Leave for several hours or overnight.

When clearing gemstone necklaces use dry salt, rather than salt water, as the water solution will quickly deteriorate the cord that gemstone chips or beads are strung upon. Dry salt or salt water will also tarnish silver settings for gemstone and crystal jewelry; they'll need to be polished afterwards. Use sea salt rather than table salt, as table salt contains aluminum and chemicals. Sea salt is available very cheaply by the pound at most health food stores. For those who live near the ocean, salt water can be brought from the beach in a jar. The gentlest way to clear crystals and stones with salt water is to wash them directly in the ocean. Hold them tightly to prevent the waves from taking them away.

Stones can also be cleared by placing them in sunlight or in moonlight, in the rain, or by burying them for a time in the Earth. Bright sun clears stones beautifully in an hour, but is detrimental to some colored gemstones that may fade. Pink or purple stones like Amethyst, Ametrine, Rose Quartz, and Kunzite, and Fluorite in all colors fade quickly in the sun. So do some light blue crystalline ones like Celestite and Aquamarine, and darker ones like Smoky Quartz. Stones can be left outdoors on full moon nights for clearing; fading is not a problem, but the stones clear less quickly and less effectively.

Try hanging gemstones from the branches of a tree in the rain, day or night, for a gentle way of clearing and cleansing them.

Stones can also be buried in the ground and left there for a period of time, which is especially good for highly overloaded healing tools. Place them with an aboveground marker so that you can find them again, or put them outdoors in a flowerpot filled with soil. (A badly overloaded stone can actually harm a plant.) Leave the stone in the Earth for a full moon cycle, from Dark Moon to Dark Moon, for complete clearing. Some stones will clear in less time, say in three days, while others may actually take longer than a month. Use this for stones that have absorbed serious negativity or pain over a long period of time.

Various herbs can also be used to clear crystals and gemstones. The herbs can either be used dry or burned for their smoke. Stones may be buried in dry herbs such as rose petals, sage, cedar, or frankincense. This is similar to using dry sea salt and is done in the same way. Rose petals may take a long time for clearing, but they will leave gemstones and crystals with a lovely soft energy. Rose Quartz and Kunzite especially feel good when cleared with dry rose petals. Dry sage or cedar are stronger herbs and are more effective for clearing stones, but still take longer than sea salt.

When herbs are burned and gemstones are passed through their smoke, the process is called smudging. Smudging with sage or cedar is a highly effective way of clearing and cleansing crystals and healing gemstones. Smudging oneself is also a good method of energy clearing and self-healing. The herbs can be found tied into smudge sticks at health food stores, herb stores, and Native American centers. Be careful that smudge sticks do not drop burning sparks, and that they are put out completely with water after using them.

My own preferred way to clear stones is under a pyramid. These can be made of glass, copper, plastic, or cardboard as long as the proportions are correct. They are sold in meta-physical stores. Books are available on how to make your own. Pyramids clear stones less quickly than sea salt does, but they also do not rot the strings of necklaces or tarnish silver. They do not fade gemstones, as sunlight may. Most stones clear overnight under a pyramid, though some in heavy use take longer. I place my jewelry and pocket stones under the pyramid on my altar each night. Because pendulums overload faster and take longer to clear, I use several pendulums and rotate them, keeping each under the pyramid for about a week before reusing. Pyramids come in all sizes, from a few inches to room-size. (Sleeping under a large one is an amazing healing experience.)

For stones to heal human (or animal or Earth) energy they must be able to transmit their highest and most positive vibration, possible only with cleared stones. No gemstone or crystal works effectively as a healing tool if its energy is not kept fully cleared. Clear a new gemstone before you program it and first use it, and clear it again frequently or after each use. This keeps the stone operating as the positive healer you first felt it to be.

Programming and Dedicating Stones

After you choose and clear your gemstone or crystal, you should dedicate and program it. This is a very simple process. Hold the stone in your hand, or touch it if it is too large to hold, and sense its energy. With the stone newly cleared, the energy will feel stronger and even more appealing than before. As you sense this energy and appreciate it, ask quietly to be connected to the deva of the crystal or gem. Though not animate, stones are living things and the deva of the piece is the stone's life force energy. Remember that every living thing including gemstones is a part of Goddess, and stones are part of the Earth. You may or may not be aware of the stone's living presence.

Once you feel you have sensed what you can from the energy, think of what you will use the stone for. Will you use it for healing? For healing yourself or others? For healing your bad back, healing your insomnia, healing your depression? Do you want the gemstone to be an energy balancer or to protect your energy? Think of these uses, general or specific, then ask the gemstone if it is willing to act in the way you wish. You will have some idea if there is a yes or no response. The crystal's energy may increase with a yes or seem to disappear with a no. If you use a pendulum, you may find your responses that way. I usually ask my stones for a broad range of function, rather than a specific use. I use most of my stones primarily for healing, and some of them (especially large ones in my home) for protection.

If the stone accepts your intent, state in your mind that it be so. If you are Wiccan the term is "And so it is" or "So mote it be." Placing intent into a gemstone is not part of any religion. What you have just done with the gemstone is to "program" it, like programming a computer. If the stone seems to refuse your intent, sense it more deeply and ask what it will do for you. You may be surprised at the response, but it will always be something you need. The life force, deva, or Goddess in the stone has an intelligence of its own, an awareness that led that particular gemstone or crystal to you. Accept the intent of the stone, agree to the intent, and thank the stone for coming into your life. In this case the stone or crystal has chosen its own programming.

If you wish to change the programming of a crystal or gemstone, first clear it thoroughly in sea salt for a longer than ordinary time. Then repeat the programming process above. Tell the energy of the stone that you wish to change its programming or its job. Reprogram it for your new intent. If you give the stone away to someone else, the new owner will reprogram the stone. Again, sense the agreement of the life force of the stone and work with it rather than against it. A stone will hold its programming until you or someone else decides to change it.

Once a stone is programmed, it is important to protect its energy from being interfered with in any way. Gemstones and crystals dissolve negative energy, but occasionally negative energy can attach to them for a while. This may result in the stone becoming ineffective as a pendulum or healing tool; it even may transmit negative energy to the user. If this happens, it is generally only temporary—gemstones and crystals do not hold onto negativity—but it is best to prevent the negative energy from happening at all. This process is called "dedicating." Once you have programmed your newly cleared stone, dedicating it can be done in one of several ways.

In the simplest method, hold the stone in your hand and sense its energy and life force. State clearly in your mind: "Only the most positive high-level energy may work through this healing tool." Focus on that intent for a while, then end your sensing (meditation) with "So mote it be" or "And so it is" as before. The stone is now dedicated, but you may take the process further.

If you use a meditation or Goddess altar, do your programming and dedicating in front of it, and call on the protection of the four directions and the four elements for the stone. You may do this by using a candle for fire/south, a bowl of water or salt water for water/west, incense smoke for air/east, and a Clear Quartz crystal for Earth/north. At each direction state, "I dedicate this stone to the protection of the north (then south, east, west)." At the north, touch your stone to the Clear Quartz; at the south, pass it quickly above the candle flame; at the east, pass it through the incense smoke; and at the west, dip it into the bowl of water or sprinkle it with a few water drops.

You may also choose to dedicate your stone or crystal to a specific healing energy, for example, to a Goddess of healing. There are many healing Goddesses, including Isis, Yemaya, Ix Chel, Diana, and White Buffalo Calf Woman. I dedicate my gemstones to Brede, the Celtic Bridgit, who was The Maiden,

healing Goddess of pre-Christian Europe. For st̲
grammed for protection, Hecate or Kali are strong pro
Goddesses. You can also dedicate your crystals and geṉ
Mary or to a saint. Stones can be dedicated to your spi̲
guide, guardian angel, or totem animal. You can ask the entity
who protects and teaches you to protect your gemstone healing
tools as well. I like to rededicate my stones occasionally.

If you have Reiki training, the Reiki symbols work beautifully to clear, program, and dedicate stones and crystals. Hold
the stone in your hand, sense its energy, then focus the symbols
into them. Start with the Dai-Ko-Myo to open the gemstone's
aura, then use the Sei-He-Ki for clearing and cleansing. Next
focus on your programming intent and fix it into the stone or
crystal with the Cho-Ku-Rei. Add the Hon-Sha-Ze-Sho-Nen
for healing stones, and finish again with the Dai-Ko-Myo.
When using the Dai-Ko-Myo for the last time, ask that the
stone become self-clearing. It will not become entirely so, but
will need far less clearing than before.

The purpose of programming a crystal or gemstone is to
focus its abilities on something you specifically need, thereby
magnifying the stone's intent through your own. The purpose
of dedicating the stone to a high-level healing energy or
Goddess is to protect it from interference from negativity. A
crystal or stone that is programmed and dedicated in these
ways becomes much more powerful and useful as a tool.

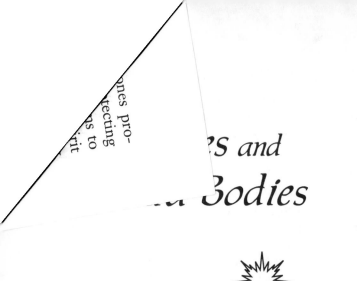

?s and

...a Bodies

*H*uman energy ends with our physical bodies, but it does not begin there. The aura is a layered electrical field surrounding the physical body, and most of what it means to be human is contained in these electrical layers. Most healers are presently aware of four aura bodies: the physical or etheric double; the emotional body; the mental body (two levels, the rational and intuitive mind); and the spiritual body (three levels). Energy work until now has been based on knowledge of these four bodies that are the beginning point for metaphysical healing of all types. To be effective, healing must normalize the aura layer that is the aberrant source of a dis-ease; physical body healing alone is not enough for permanent change. The human energy field, however, is far more complex than these four bodies.

Each of the bodies and aura levels also connects and feeds into an outer aura body layer. The emotional body connects to the astral twin, the part of consciousness that travels in meditation, psychic healing, or out-of-body experience. The mental body connects to the Body of Light or light body, which in turn connects the individual mind to the Earth grid (collective planetary mind), the galactic grid (other-planetary consciousness), and the universal grid (Goddess within or the Nonvoid). The mental body is the first of the aura bodies that continues beyond death.

The three spiritual body levels connect to outer aura layers that become the core soul. These design the other bodies below them, including the physical body, and create the blueprints for the current lifetime. These template levels comprise the actual soul. They do not end with physical death, but become the source energy of numerous incarnations. The first level, the Etheric template (not the etheric double) creates the physical body for this lifetime and maintains its existence and health. The second level, the Celestial body, is the template for the emotional self, including the astral plane and emotional body. The third level, the Ketheric body, creates the template for all the mental body levels.

Until recently these outer bodies and levels were beyond the reach of human healing. Today, however, with human psychic ability increasing (beginning the reconnection of twelve-strand DNA) and the planet's own energy expansion with the Earth changes, it is possible to access these outer bodies for profound changes and soul-level healing. The outer levels are accessed through the chakras, using the well-known kundalini chakras on the etheric double to reach other lines of chakras located on the emotional and mental bodies. The series of chakras on the emotional body, called the hara line, is primary to this increased access.

What does this mean in terms of gemstone healing? Traditionally gemstones have been used to heal the kundalini chakras on the physical body aura level, the level also known as the etheric double. (They have been secondarily and less used to balance the closest-to-physical aura bodies, , emotional, mental, and spiritual aura layers.) The ...al-etheric level is the energy layer closest to the dense physical body. Most people who work with stones know the etheric double kundalini chakras and how to match gemstone colors to them for healing.

Diagram 1
The Aura Body Levels[1]

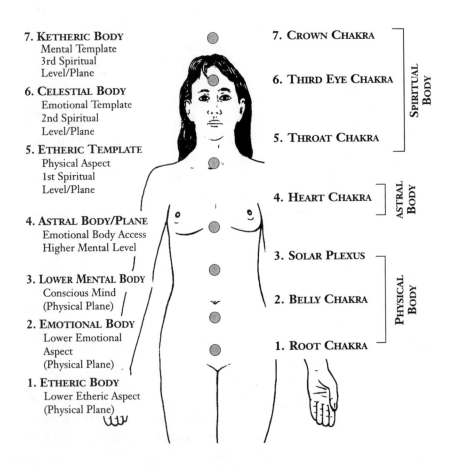

7. KETHERIC BODY
Mental Template
3rd Spiritual
Level/Plane

6. CELESTIAL BODY
Emotional Template
2nd Spiritual
Level/Plane

5. ETHERIC TEMPLATE
Physical Aspect
1st Spiritual
Level/Plane

4. ASTRAL BODY/PLANE
Emotional Body Access
Higher Mental Level

3. LOWER MENTAL BODY
Conscious Mind
(Physical Plane)

2. EMOTIONAL BODY
Lower Emotional
Aspect
(Physical Plane)

1. ETHERIC BODY
Lower Etheric Aspect
(Physical Plane)

7. CROWN CHAKRA

6. THIRD EYE CHAKRA

5. THROAT CHAKRA

SPIRITUAL BODY

4. HEART CHAKRA

ASTRAL BODY

3. SOLAR PLEXUS

2. BELLY CHAKRA

1. ROOT CHAKRA

PHYSICAL BODY

Today, however, we can go higher into the aura energy field with gemstones. They work on the emotional body level, accessing the chakras there. These emotional body hara line chakras in turn access the outer aura bodies, as well as act as a bridge between the outer bodies and the physical self. Gemstones today do much more to heal people than they did in the past, because of this shift from the kundalini to the hara line. The gemstone listings in this book reflect hara line uses for many or most of the stones.

The benefit of this is profound. In a very simple example, instead of healing a woman's migraine at only the physical level, the healing reaches the source of all her migraines. The cause may be at her etheric double throat chakra (kundalini line, traditional chakras) where she has withheld things she needs to say in this lifetime. The cause may also be from things she couldn't say in a past lifetime, or from a series of past lifetimes that have resulted in core soul damage which manifests repeatedly through her many incarnations. Healing from the hara line, using gemstones that affect that line, can reach into the Etheric template level of the throat chakra (spiritual core soul level) and heal all the past lives and the core soul damage. Not only is the woman's immediate migraine gone, but so are all her migraines through this lifetime and for all her incarnations to come. Migraines are no longer a part of her soul's blueprint. To accomplish this, gemstones are used in the ways that they have always been used, but because human energy (DNA) is now being repaired, access to healing the outer aura bodies and the results are greatly magnified. We are only at the beginning of the potential.

The next sections deal with the chakras on both the kundalini/etheric double and the hara/emotional body lines. Gemstones work through these chakras to reach the aura bodies and accomplish core soul healing.

The
Kundalini Chakras

*T*he kundalini chakras are located on the etheric double aura level, also known as the physical body aura. The etheric double is the energy layer closest to the dense physical body and considered its mirror twin. Dis-ease will manifest in the etheric double before it reaches the physical body and also can be healed and removed from the body at that place. The kundalini central channel, called the Sushumna, runs vertically up and down the center of the human body at the etheric double level. Beside and crisscrossing the central channel are two smaller channels, the Ida and Pingala. These begin at the root center (at the tailbone) and end at the left and right nostril. The seven chakras with body correspondences are located on the Sushumna in the loops between where Ida and Pingala cross. The energy movement of the two winding channels is reminiscent of the shape of our current two-strand DNA molecule. Energy rises through the kundalini chakras along these channels.

In ancient and modern traditions, spiritual development has always begun with bringing energy through the kundalini channels to open, develop, and clear the chakras. This discipline is the source of yoga, meditation, and most psychic opening work. As the chakras fill with energy, they are cleared of obstructions and healed, bringing increased physical health and psychic growth. Energy moves upward through the chakras, the seven energy centers, from the root to the crown, the physical to spiritual levels. Each ascending chakra measures development in human growth, as well as a portion of physical anatomy and health. Each ascending chakra also connects to a level of the four aura bodies.

The first three chakras—the root, belly, and solar plexus—are linked to physical body survival. The root connects to the etheric double–physical body aura layer. The belly chakra accesses the emotional body on its closest-to-physical level, and the solar plexus links to the lower level of the mental body, the conscious rational mind. The next three—the heart, throat, and brow—define the higher human needs of the intuitive mind and basic spirituality. They are the first entrances into the outer aura bodies.

The heart center is the higher mental body level, the intuitive creative mind. It offers access to the astral body twin and the astral plane (through the hara line thymus chakra just above it). The throat chakra is the seat of communication on many levels and also accesses the Etheric template level which is the physical body's blueprint. The throat is the first level of the spiritual body. The brow chakra, second spiritual body layer, is the human psychic center. Its access to the outer levels is the Celestial body, the template for the emotional self. The seventh center, the crown, is purely spiritual, the highest of the three spiritual levels of the four bodies. Its outer body

Diagram 2
The Etheric Double and Galactic Chakras[2]

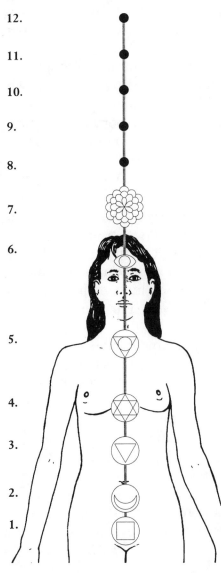

12.   **THE UNIVERSE**

11.   **GALACTIC ACCESS**

10.   **SOLAR SYSTEM ACCESS**

9.   **GRID WORK, EARTH STEWARDSHIP**
Outside earth Atmosphere as far away as the Moon

8.   **(TRANSPERSONAL POINT) INVISIBLE REALMS**
Inches to a few feet beyond body

7.   **CROWN CHAKRA**
Beyond-physical identity

6.   **BROW/THIRD EYE CHAKRA**
Vision beyond 3-D

5.   **THROAT CHAKRA**
Speaking, Truth

4.   **HEART CHAKRA**
Compassion, Connectedness

3.   **SOLAR PLEXUS CHAKRA**
Perceptual feeling

2.   **BELLY CHAKRA**
Sexuality, Creativity

1.   **ROOT CHAKRA**
Survival, Core identity

connection accesses the Ketheric body, the blueprint for the mental body, Light Body, and the mental grids.

The above are the outer body extensions of the seven major chakras and the four bodies (physical, emotional, mental, and spiritual). They may be new information for many healers, but most people have knowledge of the kundalini chakras themselves, without their aura body access links. In the past, most or all gemstone healing was based on simply balancing and clearing the kundalini chakras. I will list these chakras below as simply and briefly as possible. Pay particular attention to their colors, as they match the colors of the healing stones for each center.

The chakras begin at the base of the spine and finish at the top of the head. Though fixed in the central spinal column (the Sushumna), they are located on both the front and back of the body, and work through it. The first center is the root chakra, represented by the color red, located at the tailbone or coccyx in back and pubic bone at the body's front. This center holds the basic needs of survival, security and safety, and the ability to be grounded into earthplane existence in a body.[3] In the body, root body parts include the hips, legs, lower back, rectum, vagina, and uterus. The root chakra connects to the etheric double aura, and red gemstones heal and balance it.

Next is the belly chakra, located between the pubic bone and the navel and also rooted in the spine. Orange is the color for this center, and orange gemstones. The basic needs for this center are for sexuality, self-esteem as personal power, and power in the world. This center accesses the lowest level of the emotional bod, and houses one's unhealed inner child. Images of both this life and past life traumas are stored here, and the ability to let go of old emotions is based at this chakra. Belly chakra body parts include the ovaries, uterus, fallopian tubes, pelvis, lumbar spine, kidneys, bladder, and large intestine.

The solar plexus is the third chakra, located at the level of the lowest ribs. Its color is yellow, and the center is the body's receiver, distributor, and processor of energy and perceptual feeling. It is the lower layer of the mental body, representing the conscious and rational mind. Self-confidence and survival intuition, business and math sense, and material-level learning ability are focused here, as well as self-empowerment and the will. Body parts for this chakra include the stomach, liver, gall bladder, pancreas, and small intestine.

The second mental body chakra, the center of the creative and intuitive mind, is located at the heart. This is also the chakra connecting body and mind with spirit; it is located behind the breastbone in front and on the spine between the shoulder blades in back. The heart chakra directs one's ability to love oneself and others, to give and to receive. Two gem-stone colors represent this center: pink and green; green is the traditional color. Almost everyone today seems to have a hard, hurt, or broken heart, and it is no accident that heart dis-ease is the number one killer in America. Deep heart hurts can result in aura obstructions called heart scars. When these release, they raise quantities of old pain but free the heart for softening, healing, and new growth. Body parts for this center include the heart, lungs, circulatory system, shoulders, and the upper back.

The final three chakras comprise the spiritual body aura: the throat, brow, and crown centers. The throat chakra, located in the V of the collarbone at the lower neck, is represented by light blue color and by light blue healing stones. This is women's center of communication, expression, hearing (including psychic hearing), receiving others, and creativity. It contains and has access to the Etheric template, the blueprint of the physical body. This is possibly the most complex of the chakras, as every possibility for change, transformation, and

healing are located here, including healing one's ~~\~~
the past through karmic release. The throat is where ~~\~~
stored and finally let go of. Body parts for this center in
the throat, neck, jaw and teeth, ears and hearing, and
thyroid gland.

The indigo sixth chakra, located above the physical eyes
on the center of the forehead, is called the brow chakra, or
third eye. This is the place of seeing beyond physical realities
into the psychic realm for an understanding of nonphysical
truth. The chakra is the second spiritual aura body layer and
contains access to the Celestial body template. I define this
center as the place of Goddess within or the Buddhist
Nonvoid, and the crown chakra as Goddess herself or the
Void. Body parts for this center include the eyes, face, brain,
lymphatic, and endocrine systems.

The crown is the seventh kundalini chakra, located just
behind the top of the skull. Its color is described as violet, or
white with a golden core, and it is the third spiritual body level
with access to the Ketheric template. The center is women's
connection with Goddess and the Void, the place where life
animates the physical body. The silver cord that connects the
aura bodies extends from the crown, and the crown's contin-
uation leads outward from the spiritual body to the outer
bodies, the Body of Light and the oversoul. The soul comes
into the body through the crown at birth and leaves from the
crown at death. This is the seat where one is aware of having
a beyond-physical identity and a part in the universal Goddess
plan. Body parts for the crown chakra include the central
nervous system and the spine.

In one further comment on the kundalini line, Barbara
Marciniak describes the development of five new centers
beyond the crown. This eventual total of twelve chakras will
match the future reconnection of the twelve DNA strands.

along the straight central line of the
om the individual to the universe. They
nd have no physical coordinates. Her
invisible psychic realities beyond the
d a few inches to a few feet over the
d as far outside Earth's atmosphere
the individual to the energy grid of the
g a human being a caretaker and steward for the
The tenth center offers access to all the information of Earth's solar system; the eleventh to Earth's galaxy; and the twelfth chakra gives access to the rest of the planets, with information on deep space and the universe.[4] Through the future development of these centers, we will truly become the interplanetary Be-ings we were meant to be.

The
Hara Line

*E*nergy channels and chakra systems similar to the etheric double kundalini line exist on the other aura body levels. Until recently, most healers have not had access to or awareness of these other systems. Some people have now begun to notice the opening of new chakras, however, and are gaining awareness of another chakra series. I have named this astral/emotional body energy system the hara line, from Barbara Brennan's description of a three-chakra "Haric Level."[5] Her line and three centers match my perception, but I see a far more developed system of thirteen chakras.

The hara line holds and maintains our life purpose, why we have incarnated for this lifetime. Clear understanding of this purpose leads to productivity, fulfillment, and peace of mind in one's life. Energy blockage on this emotional body hara level obstructs our intentions and accomplishments and our awareness of this purpose. More and more, the emotional body comes to the forefront as central to any level of healing, from the physical body to the core soul. As with the kundalini line, the hara chakras have color coordinates that match the colored gemstones. Access to the chakras and their connecting bodies can be made with gemstone energy. The hara level is vitally important for today's healers and healing.

The first hara chakra is a clear-colored (all colors, no color) center above the head, which I call the transpersonal point. It is a chakra familiar to many women who have placed it on the kundalini channel. This is the soul's first manifestation into matter, the first opening of energy from the Goddess/Void. It carries the individual's reason to incarnate into her body, mind, emotions, and spirit. The transpersonal point separates the soul from its Goddess source, giving it a personal reality and a life on Earth. Other names for this center include the Soul Star. Ch'i Kung calls it the source of Heavenly Ch'i. Some clear gemstones activate this center.

Next is a pair of silver chakra centers located behind the eyes. I call these vision chakras. The eyes can be used as lasers in healing, as well as for visualization and for manifesting our needs through visualization. They are considered minor centers but are important for psychic healers. Some of the grey, iridescent, and silvery gemstones open and develop these chakras.

The causal body chakra follows, located in the base of the skull at the back where the neck meets the head. Some healers see this very major center as a light silvery blue, while others perceive it as resembling crimson yarn wrapped around a golden skein. Gemstones for this center include both crimson and silver-blue. The causal body is described as all-potential (the Nonvoid or Goddess within) and the transformer of nonphysical information/light into consciousness, as in channeling, automatic writing, and working with spirit guides. The chakra must be activated and balanced to bring mental commitment to one's life purpose, but this should be done only

Diagram 3
The Hara Line

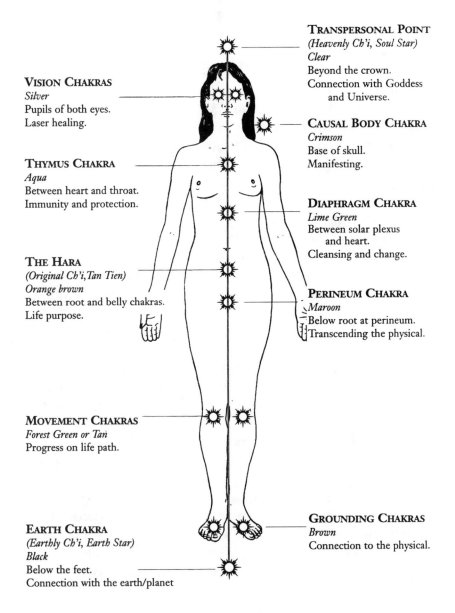

TRANSPERSONAL POINT
(Heavenly Ch'i, Soul Star)
Clear
Beyond the crown.
Connection with Goddess
and Universe.

VISION CHAKRAS
Silver
Pupils of both eyes.
Laser healing.

CAUSAL BODY CHAKRA
Crimson
Base of skull.
Manifesting.

THYMUS CHAKRA
Aqua
Between heart and throat.
Immunity and protection.

DIAPHRAGM CHAKRA
Lime Green
Between solar plexus
and heart.
Cleansing and change.

THE HARA
(Original Ch'i, Tan Tien)
Orange brown
Between root and belly chakras.
Life purpose.

PERINEUM CHAKRA
Maroon
Below root at perineum.
Transcending the physical.

MOVEMENT CHAKRAS
Forest Green or Tan
Progress on life path.

GROUNDING CHAKRAS
Brown
Connection to the physical.

EARTH CHAKRA
(Earthly Ch'i, Earth Star)
Black
Below the feet.
Connection with the earth/planet

with all the hara line chakras together. Causal body activation manifests one's spiritual life purpose, as embodied in the entire hara line, into earthplane, physical reality.

The next hara line chakra, also a major one, is the thymus chakra. I perceive this center's color as aqua or aquamarine, and I see it as connecting the hara line and emotional body to the kundalini line and etheric double. The center connects our emotions to our physical body. On the physical level, this chakra protects the immune system, which is clearly effected by the emotions, and on an emotional level is our wish to live and maintain this incarnation. The center holds our drive and passion to fulfill the task we incarnated to accomplish in this lifetime. It is obviously a vital center, central to most of today's healing issues and dis-ease sources.

You can find the thymus chakra. It is located on the chest, between and about three inches above the nipples on the breastbone. When you find it, you will know immediately; it is painful and sensitive to pressure. Gently pressing this point "brings oneself wholeheartedly awake to the grief we have carried for so long and the vastness which awaits a merciful awareness."[6] Meditating on the sensations that come while touching this point opens and releases grief (which may include anger, resentment, fear, or other feelings). Aqua gemstones also activate this center, and much healing happens along the way.

Next, below the thymus is the diaphragm chakra, at the level of the physical diaphragm muscle, just above the solar plexus. Its color is lime green, and it is activated by some of the green or yellow green gemstones. I perceive this center as providing a clearing and detoxification of any obstructions to the fulfillment of one's life purpose. This is a cleansing of the entire hara line and can be a quite intense, deep emotional purging. Healers who have experienced this chakra have called it the "garbage chakra" or the "vomit chakra." The process is ultimately positive but may not seem so at the time. Go through it by simply allowing it to happen. Watch the sensations and let them go, not fighting, resisting, or trying to change them. Welcome the clearing and send love.

The next primary center on the hara line is the hara chakra, or the hara itself. Known in Asia from ancient times, it is located about two and a half inches below the navel, above the kundalini belly chakra. Its color is golden to orange brown but may deepen in healing, even turning hot and red. In Asia, all energy work starts and ends at this center, which is the source of incarnation and the place that the life force emanates from. The hara chakra connects one's will to live with the life-sustaining energy of the Earth at the Earth chakra (see below). Strength, power, life force, and regenerative ability also originate from this center when the chakra is fully grounded to the Earth.

The deep ruby or maroon perineum chakra is next. This energy point is located (on the emotional body) between the openings of the vagina and the anus, where episiotomies are performed in childbirth. This is the energy gate through which the Earth Ch'i life force is brought into the body and held for distribution at the hara center. In Ch'i Kung it is called "the gateway of life and death." The perineum is the place of activating and anchoring one's life intention and purpose into physical plane reality. Only a few gemstones activate this chakra.

A pair of small chakras is located behind the knees. Called movement chakras, they direct one's movement forward on one's life path. People who have resistance or difficulty in fulfilling their life purpose may have pain in their knees, and the color-matching gemstones are usually tan or forest green. Below the knee chakras, on the soles of the feet, is another chakra pair. These are called grounding chakras, and their color is brown. These chakras center one's life purpose into physical direction and manifestation.

The energy line begun at the transpersonal point moves vertically through the body and enters deep into the Earth, as deep as the person can ground herself into the planet and root her intention for being here. The chakra that roots the hara line into Goddess Earth is called the Earth chakra, or Earth Star. I see its color as shiny black, and some black gemstones help to activate it. The chakra anchors the incarnation/lifetime into earthplane reality, makes this planet one's home, and places one's life purpose into an Earthly context. This ending of the hara line is the grounding and ballast for one's lifetime and life purpose.

Besides the chakras, the hara line itself is comprised of a double flow of energy. One channel moves from the perineum chakra up the back, over the top of the head, down the face to the upper lip. In acupuncture and Ch'i Kung this channel is called the Governor Channel. The second energy flow starts at the lower lip and descends down the front of the body to end at the perineum. This is called the Conception Vessel. Auxiliary flows move energy through the legs and arms into these channels. Ch'i Kung is the ancient energy discipline that develops the hara channels and chakras, similar to the way that yoga works with the kundalini line.

The emotions are central to today's healing issues and needs, and the hara line chakras offer access to achieving profound emotional healing. Gemstones that match the hara line chakras provide direct entry into the emotional body and through it to the outer aura bodies for core soul healing. The ability to have that access is a major healing breakthrough.

Laying on
of Stones

*T*he technique of using crystals and gemstones on the receiver's body for healing is called laying on of stones. It is a powerful method of cleansing negative energy, clearing and balancing the chakras, effecting emotional release, and bringing light and healing into all the aura bodies. Cleared, programmed, and dedicated stones move the receiver's vibration into alignment with the planet and the universal grid. This results in a freeing of life force energy in the chakras and aura, a healing of the Body of Light, and a transformation of negative or dis-ease energy into health. Laying on of stones also affects the chakras on both kundalini and hara line levels.

The process may be done with clear quartz crystals only, colored gemstones only, or a combination of both. I prefer a combination. The stones may be used alone or with a hands-on healing, and again I prefer both. The stones are placed upon the receiver's body from feet to head. The healer then begins using her hands as usual, starting at the head and moving toward the feet. Use gemstones with colors matching each chakra's color, the hara chakra stones appearing between the kundalini centers. The stones can be any combination of forms—faceted, raw, tumbled, eggs, strings of beads, etc. Clear crystals can be used at any chakra, with or without colored gemstones.

Energy in this type of healing needs to move in one direction through the body, either Earth to sky or sky to Earth. If the energy is Earth to sky, all of the crystals or gemstones that have points are placed with the points turned toward the receiver's crown. The effect of this direction is to move the receiver's energy to a higher vibration or more spiritual level. If the direction is from sky to Earth, it is the opposite, with the crystals pointing toward her feet. This direction moves life force energy from crown to feet, for grounding and rooting into Earth. A number of patterns can be used for placing crystals and gemstones on the body, but following the line of the central channels is basic, all that is actually required.

To place the stones, put colored gemstones on the chakras, matching their colors to the chakra colors. Put clear crystals in the receiver's hands, above her crown, below her feet, and in a circle around her body a few inches away. The crystals around the body should point toward the receiver. Clear crystals can also be used at each chakra, surrounded by the colored gemstones. They can be placed between the kundalini chakras so that they are over the hara chakras to activate the hara line, or colored stones can be placed over the hara chakras, as well.

To begin, the receiver lies on her back on a padded floor or massage table, with pillows under her head and knees for comfort. The healer may use a chair or stand beside a massage table but needs to be able to move about freely. The space should be quiet, comfortable, warm, and not likely to be disturbed. The stones need to be cleared before using them—this is very important. Use only stones that have been dedicated to positive energy and programmed for healing. Invite the participant's spirit guides and angels into the session.

Start by placing the crystals below the receiver's feet, in her hands, and above her head. Then go chakra by chakra, moving from feet to crown. Spread the stones where you can reach them and select what goes on each center. There may be stones you do not use for a particular person, and stones that are drawn to a chakra where their colors don't logically match. Let yourself be guided; there are no real rules. A stone whose energy is not needed for the session or is inappropriate for the receiver's energy will roll right off or roll to another place where it is better utilized. Allow this to occur. If you "forget" to place a stone, it is because its energy is not useful for that person or healing. If the receiver says a stone feels uncomfortable take it off; the energy isn't right for her needs.

When the stones are all in place, the healer has two options. She can next go to the receiver's head and begin a hands-on healing. She must place her hands carefully so that she does not scatter the stones. Her other choice is to sit beside the receiver quietly and simply wait, allowing the stones and spirit guides to do the healing. As the receiver's chakras and aura absorb and are balanced by the crystal and gem energies, the stones begin to roll off one by one. The receiver may say that something now feels uncomfortable or feels finished; move that stone from her body. Sometimes all the stones seem to jump off at once, though the receiver is lying perfectly still. It can startle and is often funny when this happens. Do not replace them.

When all the stones are off, or you or the receiver feel finished with those that remain, the healing is over. Allow the receiver to lie quietly for a while without the stones. While she is doing this, the healer can gather up the stones from the table and floor and clear them again before putting them away.

Clearing the stones before and after each healing is necessary. After clearing, I keep mine in a protective pouch.

A laying-on-of-stones healing can be quite intense. There is often a major energy shift during this type of healing. More frequent emotional releases, past-life and this-life trauma openings, and other transformative events happen when gemstones and crystals are used than would occur without them. The healer's role in this is to wait for the release to end and to be entirely nonjudgmental. After a session, there may also be a physical and emotional detoxification process that can continue for up to a week. Be aware of what is happening and, again, allow it. The changes are always positive and are usually gentle.

A directory of healing gemstones follows. Asterisks have been placed by those stones most commonly used.

Notes

1 Barbara Ann Brennan, *Hands of Light: A Guide to Healing through the Human Energy Field* (New York: Bantam Books, 1987), 47.

2 Barbara Marciniak, *Bringers of the Dawn: Teachings from the Pleiadians* (Santa Fe, N.M.: Bear & Co., 1992), 55–56; and Barbara Marciniak, *Earth: Pleiadian Keys to the Living Librar*, (Santa Fe, N.M.: Bear & Co., 1995), 34–35.

3 The analysis of Carolyn Myss influences this version of the seven chakras. See C. Norman Shealy, MD, and Carolyn M. Myss, MA, *The Creation of Health: The Emotional, Psychological and Spiritual Responses that Promote Health and Healing* (Walpole, N.H.: Stillpoint Publishing, 1993), 93–119.

4 Barbara Marciniak, *Bringers of the Dawn* 55–56, and *Earth*, 34–35.

5 Barbara Ann Brennan, *Light Emerging: The Journey of Personal Healing* (New York: Bantam Books, 1993), 29.

6 Stephen Levine, *Healing into Life and Death* (New York: Anchor Books, 1987), 116–117.

Gemstone Listings

*Agate–Blue Lace
※

Color: Blue and white
Chakra: Throat

- Makes self-expression easier, aids speaking out, aids speaking and validating one's emotional truths
- Offers courage, aids shyness and tendency towards self-effacement
- Clears the throat chakra; programs the etheric body for creative work; heals laryngitis, sore throats, hoarseness; soothes and calms; opens the voice

Agate–Botswana
※

Color: Peach and white
Chakra: Heart

- Affects the heart like a stone thrown into a pool, with rings and ripples radiating out to heal old pain
- Heals heartache and heart pain layer by layer, replaces pain with joy
- Heals and warms the heart, offering comfort and security

Agate–Brown
※

Color: Brown and black
Chakra: Grounding

- Moves energy from head to feet, from spiritual levels and outer bodies into the physical
- Grounds spiritual awareness and life purpose into earth-plane action, spiritual presence in daily life
- Promotes stability of emotions and purpose; calms, centers, grounds
- Aids nausea, indigestion, and cramps

Agate–Bull's Eye

———✦———

Color: Black and white
Chakra: Earth chakra

- Grounds spirituality, moves energy from the spiritual bodies into the physical, targets spiritually expanding awareness into focused earthplane action
- Calms and concentrates a scattered life purpose, aids real earthplane achievement of worldly and incarnational goals
- Keeps one's life purpose on target, promotes focus and action on the earthplane

Agate–Crazy Lace

———✦———

Color: Black and white
Chakra: Earth chakra

- Connects Heavenly Ch'i to Earthly Ch'i, brings spiritual level energy into the entire hara line and roots it into earthplane reality and consciousness
- Clears the hara line of energy blockages, balances Earth and sky, stabilizes and grounds while elevating awareness
- Helps to clear emotional pain, helps center and focus

Agate–Dendritic

———✦———

Color: Green and clear
Chakra: Movement

- Moves energy from the outer bodies and chakras into the physical level in the head-to-feet direction
- Merges one's incarnational purpose with the Earth change needs of the planet

- Offers a focus on environmentalism, Earth awareness, and service to the Earth
- Raises mass consciousness, helps to save plant and animal species, helps to heal nature, aids activists and activism

Agate–Fire
❋

Color: Orange and white
Chakra: Hara chakra

- Brings energy from the spiritual outer bodies into the hara chakra, aids in attaining spiritual awareness of one's incarnational purpose, strengthens the ability and will to manifest one's life purpose on the earthplane
- Strengthens the will to achieve one's karmic agreements for this lifetime; aids stability, concentration and manifestation of one's life work; increases energy

Agate–Geode
❋

Color: Brown, grey, black
Chakra: Earth chakra

- Draws negativity, pain, and energy blocks through the chakra and aura layers to release them
- Suctions and vacuum-cleans aura energy, acts as a magnet for negative energy and pulls it out, grounds negative energy into the Earth while cleansing and transforming it
- Is a good tool for aura workers, massage therapists, and energy healers

Most geodes are self-clearing.

Agate–Holly Blue

Color: Blue violet
Chakra: Causal body

- Moves spiritual energy from higher levels into the physical level
- Opens and balances the causal body chakra for transmission of spiritual energy into consciousness
- Stabilizes spiritual energy moving into physical awareness
- Focuses one's life purpose and karmic learning plan for this incarnation into physical fulfillment
- Transmits higher-level information in a stepped-down way to move it into earthplane understanding
- A good aid for new channelers

Agate–Leopard Skin

Color: Pink and tan
Chakra: Heart

- Protects the heart chakra at the etheric double level only
- Brings spiritual energy into the heart to heal heartache and heartbreak
- Protects healers from burnout and from getting overly involved emotionally with those they heal
- Aids holding unconditional love
- Clears psychic attacks at the heart chakra level, slowly dissolves negative cords in the heart chakra, heals heart scars slowly

Think of your strongest fear; take a piece of leopard skin agate in one hand and a piece of bloodstone in the other. Focus on your fear and watch it dissolve. (I thank Joy Weaver for this exercise.)

*Agate–Moss or Montana Agate

❁

Color: Brown and clear
Chakra: Movement

- Brings energy from the outer bodies and chakras into the physical level by energy movement from head to feet
- Makes spiritual knowledge and purpose conscious on earthplane levels
- Aids in incorporating one's life purpose and spirituality into everyday action
- Aids in walking one's talk and living one's incarnational agreements, walking softly on the Earth Mother
- Helps nausea and lack of being grounded

Agate–Red-Brown

❁

Color: Brown and orange
Chakra: Belly

- Calms belly chakra activity
- Eases sexual cravings, eases longings for a child and pregnancy
- Helps premenstrual syndrome, menstrual cramps, nausea, and brings on menstrual flow
- Is generally emotionally calming; slows, warms, and stabilizes

Agate–Sand Cast

❁

Color: White, cream
Chakra: Vision

- For viewing oneself as an ancient Be-ing and life as but a moment of the greater whole
- Increases awareness of having had many lifetimes and of life beyond the body as a soul

- Provides information on the between life state
- Promotes understanding of soul structure, knowledge of one's part in the universal plan, and awareness of spirit guides, soul families, soul mates, and Goddess

Agate–Sunset
※

Color: Lavender
Chakra: Crown

- Protects the link between the crown and the outer chakras
- Aids meditation, and psychic development, is calming
- Aids dream work, dream recall, and insomnia; reduces stress
- Helps perfectionists to know when a project is finished and that everything is done well
- Prompts the feeling that everything is okay in one's world and one's deeds
- Promotes a sense of balanced achievement, reduces nervousness, aids self-confidence
- Is good for workaholics

**Amazonite*
※

Color: Aqua and white
Chakra: Thymus

- Aids ability to release emotional body grief by expressing it as creativity
- Opens the connection between the thymus/emotional body and the throat/etheric body
- Promotes the expression of emotions in order to heal and resolve them
- Aids concentration, helps in completing projects

- Is useful for writers, musicians, dancers, and nonverbal artists
- Aids calcium balance, the parathyroid and thyroid glands
- Aids alcoholism at a nutritional level

*Amber
❁

Color: Gold brown
Chakra: Hara chakra

- Stabilizes the entire hara system and emotional body
- Promotes the certainty of one's path and choices, mental and emotional strength
- Facilitates energy balancing and cleansing, all-aura healing
- Refills, protects, and repairs aura tears from too rapid emotional or karmic release
- Removes psychic attacks, lessens damage from anesthetics, or other negative agents
- Is a protective shield against taking on others' pain in healing work
- Protects against psychic attack, psychic draining, or energy intrusion by others
- Is highly calming

*Amethyst–Brazilian or Mexican
❁

Color: Purple
Chakra: Crown

- Opens conscious access to the spiritual body, promotes spiritual awareness and awakening, teaches that Be-ing does not stop with the body
- Gives conscious awareness of the soul, Goddess and infinity, awareness of other than physical levels and realms

- Introduces one's guides and angels, gives awareness of self as part of a universal plan, and self as part of Goddess
- Increases sense of responsibility, self-worth, spiritual peace
- Aids in meditation; helps insomnia, headaches, alcohol recovery
- Dis-eases of the head and brain, eases stress

Amethyst–Canadian

Color: Purple and red
Chakra: Crown

- Stabilizes the connection of soul and body, of spiritual with physical levels
- Manifests spiritual awareness in daily life, spirituality as a way of living and Be-ing, grounding spirituality into the body
- Aids in understanding the wheel of life, death, and rebirth
- Aids in the understanding of self as a part of the universe and universal whole
- Furthers the appreciation of the oneness of all life
- Aids alcohol and drug recovery, alleviates headaches and migraines, relieves stress, gives inner peace

Amethyst–Elestial

Color: Light violet
Chakra: Crown

- Opens all chakras beyond the crown and kundalini line, opens the intergalactic chakras, opens the connection with Pleiadian higher Be-ings
- Brings other-planetary help, healing, and light
- Gives protection from negative alien energy, clears energy
- Assures that "everything will be okay"
- Calms and stabilizes

Amethyst–Pink

Color: Pink
Chakra: Heart

- Opens the heart chakra for giving and receiving
- Gives positive self-image, body image, self-esteem, self-love, empowerment
- Connects heart and crown chakras for the spiritualization of one's life, one's emotions, and one's responses to others
- Promotes unconditional love and compassion, heals old and new this-life and past-life traumas, heals the emotional body and one's inner child

Amethyst–Rutile

Color: Purple and metallic
Chakra: Crown

- Aligns and raises the energy of the kundalini channels, clears energy flow and blockages in Ida, Pingalla, and Sushumna
- Balances and clears ch'i energy flow to brain, and central and autonomic nervous systems, clears lymphatic channels and acupuncture meridians
- Aids the understanding and healing of personal karma, brings awareness of this lifetime as one in a chain of many lifetimes
- Promotes awareness of this life's learnings and agreements as they fit into the soul's full incarnational plan

Amethyst–Smoky

Color: Purple and grey
Chakra: Earth

- Brings spiritual certainty into physical levels and conscious awareness
- Protects from psychic attacks, negative entities, and negative alien energy
- Is a gatekeeper to prevent entrance of negative energy while drawing in positive energy and help
- Aids contact with spirit guides and angels, aids in readiness for channeling, helps to ground after channeling and psychic work
- Aids conscious spiritual growth, meditation

Ametrine

Color: Purple and gold
Chakra: Crown

- Stabilizes the balance between spirituality and daily life, aids in bringing spiritual values and abilities into daily use, supports spirituality as a way of life
- Helps psychic opening and development, astral projection, working with spirit guides, meditation
- Balances inward with outward energy flows

Andean Opal

Color: Aqua and grey
Chakra: Thymus

- Increases awareness of and healing of the Earth, compassion for the planet and all that lives

- Helps oneself, the Earth, and all species through the Earth changes
- Aids Earth healers and their work, helps individuals who manifest Earth change energy and trauma in their bodies and emotions
- Helps emotional body healing
- Supports inner growth and transitions
- Heals grief and loss, gives inner peace.

A tumbled piece resembles the Earth as viewed from space.

*Angelite

Color: Light blue
Chakra: Throat

- Stabilizes emotions and the physical and emotional bodies
- Is a calmative
- Enhances creativity and psychic ability, voice channeling, ability to speak out for oneself and to teach or perform
- Aids connection with spirit guides and angels and increases the ability to psychically hear and work with them
- Increases the angelic protection to oneself and one's home
- Aids rebirthing, dispels anger, aids forgiveness and self-forgiveness, facilitates telepathic sending and receiving with people and pets

Apatite–Blue

Color: Deep aqua
Chakra: Thymus

- Detoxes suffering from the thymus chakra and emotional body "not my pain but the world's pain," aids those who feel the Earth's emotions in their bodies

- Releases the idea of deserving to suffer, releases grief for oneself and the state of the world
- Aids letting go of pain to accept peace and joy, to appreciate the beauty of the Earth
- Aids the immune system

Apatite–Yellow
※

Color: Yellow green
Chakra: Diaphragm

- Detoxifies negative emotions relating to self-image: feeling inadequate, ugly, shy, shamed, guilty
- Releases karmic guilt and the "Cross of St. Michael"; releases karmic suffering; releases the feeling that one deserves pain, poverty, and misfortune
- Allows one to accept love, comfort, support, and self-love
- Improves body image, aids in healing protective obesity, furthers the ability to assimilate
- Cleanses the lymphatic, glandular, and meridian systems

Aphrodite
※

Color: Pink
Chakra: Heart

- Opens you to receive love and support from a significant other
- Increases ability to give emotionally to a lover, to draw a mate to you, to find your twin soul relationship, to form a relationship
- Helps you achieve fidelity in relationship, to form trust and cooperation with a mate

t scars and the emotional body

ımaging effects of failed relationships from this

Apophyllite–Aqua

—☼—

Color: Light aqua
Chakra: Thymus

- Heals grief and clears it from the emotional body, brings inner peace and ability to accept and release loss and emotional pain
- Increases self-forgiveness, forgiveness of others, awareness of self and others as spiritual Be-ings; increases awareness that the body is only temporary and only a small part of the life of the soul
- Opens conscious connection to the astral body twin, the Light Body, and oversoul
- Encourages acceptance, allowing the return of joy, the feeling that "it's okay"

Apophyllite–Clear

—☼—

Color: Clear
Chakra: Causal body

- Brings spiritual consciousness to physical level awareness, unifies and aligns the aura bodies, increases awareness of oneself as a spiritual Be-ing of far greater magnitude than earthplane level only
- Brings astral twin into physical-etheric body level, opens connection to Light Body and oversoul, heals soul fragmentation, aids soul retrieval
- Helps to repair twelve-strand DNA, fills aura and aura bodies with light, joy

Aqua Aura Crystal

☼

Color: Blue, iridescent
Chakra: Throat

- Brings light into the throat chakra, heals the ability to feel and express emotions, increases awareness of inner truth, heals inability to speak out and fear of speaking out
- Heals karmic structural damage to the throat chakra
- Aids telepathy and empathy, opens awareness of one's spiritual life

Also see Silver Aura Crystal.

*Aquamarine

☼

M

Color: Aqua
Chakra: Thymus

- Fills hara line with healing light that reaches the kundalini line via the thymus, connects hara and kundalini channels and chakras
- Comforts in times of intense physical, emotional and karmic release; supports one through the process
- Aids a life path of service; shields and protects
- Ocean Goddess energy; reminds of the love and caring of the Goddess through times of change and in one's life path and purpose
- Aids communication with spirit guides and angels, aids connection with oversoul, promotes spiritual and psychic awareness
- Brings about core soul repair and healing, aids soul retrieval, heals deeply at all levels

Aragonite

Color: Grey and lavender
Chakra: Vision

- Promotes the return to reality after euphoric states
- Furthers grounding into truth, bursts the bubble of false-hood; aids seeing what is real—like it or not
- Overcomes illusions and delusions, forces one to face the unvarnished truth and to accept reality

Avalonite (Blue Druzy Chalcedony)

Color: Blue violet
Chakra: Third eye

- Opens the mythical past known from the ancient archetypes of the collective consciousness, legends and lore, folklore and fairy tales: tales of King Arthur and Guinevere, Morgan Le Fay, druids, wisewomen, fairies, elves, and Goddesses— opens their wisdom and teaching for present-day use
- Brings awareness of the magick of the past and knowing that magick is still with us, promotes using magick now via psychic awareness, increases awareness of being of a long line of psychic/magickal women
- Aids meditation and visualization, calms and soothes, gives a feeling of security

*Aventurine–Blue

Color: Dark blue
Chakra: Third eye

- Teaches, heals, and regenerates; moves the wounded inner child from the belly chakra and heals her into the heart;

facilitates inner-child work, inner healing, and healing emotional and mental bodies

- Heals the emotions via the mind and universal Goddess mind, and Goddess within, providing access to Light Body, mental body grid, and planetary grid
- Connects with spirit guides and high-level healers, releases space junk and artifacts from the aura, releases negative entities and attachments from the aura and chakras
- Aids in karmic release and karmic healing, provides access to the Lords of Karma

Aventurine–Green

Color: Green
Chakra: Heart

- Opens the heart to others and increases trust in life
- Fosters the ability to be light hearted, and to take emotional risks
- Cleanses the heart chakra of fear, soothes physical and emotional heart pain, creates emotional safety and security
- Heals heart dis-eases, infections
- Brings about adventures in love and travel

Aventurine–Peach

Color: Peach
Chakra: Belly

- Encourages playful sexuality, encourages the conception of a child or other creative effort
- Sustains creativity or fertility from conception to birth, promotes gentle and joyful pregnancy or creative process, inspires new ideas

- Manifests new life or new art onto the earthplane; stimulates creativity of mothers, photographers, visual artists, potters, painters

*Azurite

———————————✧———————————

Color: Dark blue
Chakra: Third eye

- Acts as a third-eye counterpart of heart center dioptase, heals emotional trauma from this and past lives at the mental body level
- Evokes karmic healing of negative energy patterns brought from other lifetimes, causes intense transformation and transcendence, spurs breakthroughs when a healing process seems stuck
- Develops active and conscious connection to one's Light Body and the planetary mind grid, to the Void and Non-void
- Helps to connect with spirit guides, angels, extraplanetary helpers, Goddess
- Dissolves blocks and negativity, heals confusion
- Aids Earth healers, meditators, psychics; increases psychic healing ability and visualization

Azurite–Malachite

———————————✧———————————

Color: Green and blue
Chakra: Third eye

- Encourages emotional breakthroughs, and inner transformations, bringing karmic patterns into conscious awareness for releasing and healing

- Opens, cleanses, and releases; connects the mind and emotions
- Heals past-life traumas, heals the emotional and mental bodies

Barite
❖

Color: Peach and black
Chakra: Hara

- Clears, expands, and develops the hara chakra; clears blocks and hara hooks
- Clears obstacles to achieving one's life path
- Increases heat, ch'i, and energy; brings energy from hara line channels and grounds it safely into the hara chakra
- Conserves energy; helps those who are scattered or who have low vitality, chronic fatigue or exhaustion; aids gentle, balanced energy flow

Beryl–Golden
❖

Color: Gold, yellow
Chakra: Diaphragm

- Soothes the person exhausted from long-term healing and emotional release work
- Calms and aligns the emotional body, aids in balancing sustained changes and energy expansions
- Heals the astral body twin and brings it into the physical aura, supports weary old souls and bodhisattvas through the Earth changes
- Aids healers' burnout, helps the menopause process

For other Beryls, see Aquamarine, Emerald, Goshenite, Morganite.

Bismuth

✦

Color: metallic, multi
Chakra: None

• Manmade, and possesses no attributes for healing the aura, aura bodies or chakras

Bloodstone

✦

Color: Green and red
Chakra: Movement

• Forces one's focus onto the physical level and the earthplane, minimizes psychic perceptions and distractions
• Cleanses the blood, fosters courage in living one's life on Earth and moving forward on one's life path, prevents distractions from one's life path
• Aids earthplane achievement, offers psychic protection
Also see Jasper.

*Boji Stones

✦

Color: brown, metallic
Chakra: Grounding

• Works from the emotional body level to clear and stabilize the entire aura system
• Heals negative feelings, negative emotional patterns, and old pain
• Translates emotional changes into physical body healing; used singly bojis heal physical pain, used in pairs they open the aura and release blockages from the acupuncture meridians and human electrical system

- Promotes free flow of ch'i and balanced energy; helps heal structural-skeletal pain, arthritis, backaches, scoliosis, osteoporosis
- Aids feeling supported and nurtured by the Earth

Bronzite
—✹—

Color: Brown
Chakra: Grounding

- Aids the ability to make choices and decisions about one's life and life path, clears confusion by reducing choices to the essentials and the one choice needed for now
- Produces the resolution to follow through with one's choices regarding one's life and to keep to one's path, stimulates courage
- Is a good stone for men, a masculine energy

Calcite–Amber
—✹—

Color: Golden orange
Chakra: Hara chakra

- Intensifies the circuit of energy/ch'i through the hara line channels and chakras, stimulates the Ch'i Kung microcosmic orbit, aids in opening the hara line chakras for spiritual soul growth
- Brings light/information/ch'i from outer bodies into the physical and emotional levels
- Clears energy blockages, stabilizes soul potential and life purpose
- Heals ulcers and arthritis

Calcite–Blue

❁

Color: Light blue
Chakra: Throat

- Soothes the throat, eases the ability to speak out, heals throat center blockages and throat dis-eases, clears old this-life traumas held in the throat
- Supports peaceful assertiveness, aids shyness, promotes ability to speak one's needs
- Soothes anger, creates a readiness for peaceful change in one's life, brings inner peace and quiet within
- Contributes to beginning spiritual growth

Calcite–Bushy Creek

❁

Color: Metallic and grey
Chakra: Vision

- Facilitates using the eyes as lasers in healing; opens and focuses the vision chakras; promotes focus in one's life, one-pointed awareness and concentration
- Fine tunes psychic perception, aids the ability to scan energy and see auras and the ability to do psychic surgery

Calcite–Dog Tooth

❁

Color: White
Chakra: Vision

- Aids perception and focus, acts as a psychic surgery tool for opening the aura and clearing energy blocks

- Opens and focuses the vision chakras, facilitates using the eyes as lasers in healing, fine tunes psychic perception and visualization ability
- Aids concentration, neurological imbalances and mis-alignments
- Increases physical and psychic vision

Calcite–Green
❊

Color: Light green
Chakra: Diaphragm

- Brings a flow of light through the diaphragm chakra to "wash" and clear it
- Intensifies the cleansing of old pain and negative emotions from the emotional body, speeds clearing of negativity from the emotional body and hara line
- Detoxifies physical and emotional levels, clears pollutants and toxins from the meridian system

Calcite–Optical
❊

Color: Clear
Chakra: Vision

- Opens and clears the transpersonal point and crown for the ability to see and accept higher levels of spiritual energy
- Fills the aura with light, clears attachments and entities, opens the whole hara line and hara chakra
- Supports the vision of a spiritual reality, engenders trust in the opening and trust in the new way of seeing

*Calcite–Orange
☼

Color: Light orange
Chakra: Belly

- Soothes and heals past-life pictures of old traumas held in the belly chakra, aids in healing and releasing sexual abuse from past lives
- Aids in releasing karmic negative behaviors and personality problems resulting from past-life traumas and abuse, clears negative karmic patterns
- Heals current-life sexuality, past abuse, and being battered in this lifetime

Calcite–Pink
☼

Color: Pink
Chakra: Heart

- Rebuilds the heart chakra and emotional body after releasing old traumas
- Refills the heart with love, self-love, and light after releasing past-life and this-life pain, heals and repairs the heart after clearing heart scars
- Teaches new trust, heals the inner child
- Brings about the healed and regenerated heart, soothes and offers hope

Calcite–Red Phantom
☼

Color: Orange and red
Chakra: Root

- Provides courage and the will to live, aids in healing life-threatening dis-eases

- Inspires the courage to die and be reborn, the courage to see an incarnation through to its fulfillment and conclusion, and the courage to stay in one's body and face one's life
- Grounds, strengthens the life force and ability to survive

*Carnelian

Color:Orange
Chakra: Belly

- Stimulates, balances, and heals women's reproductive system—uterus, ovaries, fallopian tubes, cervix, vagina
- Helps alleviate premenstrual syndrome, irregular menstrual cycles, cramps
- Brings on periods; helps girls at menarche to appreciate their bodies and women to value and respect their life-making ability
- Promotes responsible sexuality, sacred sex, and planned reproduction
- Aids creativity of all sorts, raises moods, warms, aids non-inflammatory arthritis

Carnelian–Poppy

Color: Peach, pink
Chakra: Belly

- Promotes the sacredness of home and family, helps mother-child bond
- Supports new mothers and pregnancy, eases fear of parenting
- Helps infants adjust to their new bodies and accept incarnation

- Aids children who wish to leave their families, eases children's resistance to discipline
- Aids asthmatic children and adults

*Celestite
❋

Color: Light blue
Chakra: Causal body

- Heals the aura, astral body, and Light Body; aligns the bodies
- Fosters connection and ability to work with Goddesses, spirit guides, angels, nature devas, dolphin devas, ascended Be-ings
- Advances channeling; brings about information/light, core soul healing, twelve-strand DNA, psychic development, spiritual and karmic growth
- Evokes peace, manifests the element of water and the ability to flow with life

Chalcedony–Pink
❋

Color: Pink
Chakra: Heart

- Creates compassion, heart opening, and heart maturity
- Inspires honoring the oneness of all life and the sacredness of all that lives
- Fosters awareness of the suffering of others and of oneself; increases awareness of Goddess and Goddess within; aids knowing oneself as a part of the Goddess whole, a child of the Goddess
- Promotes peace and harmony within, is self-blessing
- Enhances women's self-image, a feminine energy

Chalcedony–White

Color: White, clear
Chakra: Third eye

- Brings awareness of the sacredness of all life, contributes to knowing oneself to be part of a universal plan and wholeness
- Advances spiritual growth and maturity; creates respect for sacredness in every path, respect for the Earth and all that lives on it, and respect for oneself and others as children of the Goddess
- Produces harmony within oneself and with others, promotes world peace

Chalcopyrite

Color: Metallic gold
Chakra: Solar plexus

- Aids in achieving prosperity and abundance without and within, attracts necessities and comforts
- Fosters the feeling of having everything one needs and wants, promotes the awareness of inner abundance and knowledge that abundance comes only from within
- Creates financial and material security; contributes to finding inner peace in a material world; fosters nonmaterialism, gratitude

Charoite

Color: Purple and black
Chakra: Crown

- Brings spirituality onto the earthplane level, raises Earth energy to the crown, spiritualizes daily living

- Promotes raised awareness of more than material and physical body reality, heals the body by making one aware of karma and a higher plan
- Aids responsibility, heals those who selfishly control others by making them morally aware, raises ethical level

Chrysoberyl Cat's Eye

✦

Color: Grey gold
Chakra: Vision

- Creates the ability to see as a cat sees—all the things people miss; evokes visions of other realms, dimensions, planets; promotes psychic vision
- Fosters contact with positive other-planetary healers and teachers
- Aids dream work and dream clairvoyance
- Facilitates out-of-body journeys
- Creates affinity and oneness with cats, enhances psychic communication with small cats and large ones

*Chrysocolla

✦

Color: Aqua
Chakra: Thymus

- For women's all-healing and internal physical healing, connects one with Goddess
- Creates awareness of self as a part of Goddess
- Connects thymus and throat chakras for releasing grief, sadness, and fear from the emotional body and aiding the entrance of joy, certainty, and peace
- Supports letting go, surrendering pain and worry to universal love

- Aids emotional healing from incest, rape, mastectomy, and hysterectomy (this life)
- Heals lungs, throat, heart, premenstrual syndrome, cramps, inflammations

Chrysoprase
※

Color: Green
Chakra: Heart

- Soothes heartache and loneliness, fosters emotional balance, conflict resolution, inner peace, inner strength
- Provides courage in facing real emotions, opens and heals old traumas and grief
- Creates trust in Goddess, facilitates learning to flow with life and change, reduces fear

Cinnabar Wood
※

Color: Red
Chakra: Root

- Stimulates the life force and will to live, increases interest in one's life and surroundings
- Increases one's drive to succeed and to reproduce, creates awareness of biological clock and awareness of time passing and one's life passing with it
- Promotes longevity, warms the body, raises mood, prevents suicide, deters senility
- Increases alertness, focuses on earthplane living rather than spiritual awareness

Citrine–Heat Created

Color: Yellow
Chakra: Solar plexus

- Aids assimilation and digestion of energy, food, ideas
- Helps the urinary tract, stimulates the mind and energy, moves energy upward from solar plexus to open blockages in the upper chakras
- Detoxifies the kundalini channels, raises psychic ability by magnifying it, aids in understanding psychic information, and controlling astral projection
- Fosters self-awareness, alertness

*Citrine–Natural

Color: Gold
Chakra: Solar plexus

- Cleanses and detoxifies the kundalini line and emotional body
- Regenerates tissue, balances the spine on meridian and energy levels by balancing ch'i movement through the central nervous system
- Clears, expands and aligns the aura bodies; heals, opens, and aligns etheric, emotional, and mental levels; opens the light body; fills aura with light and clarity
- Stimulates intellect and mental activity
- Aids urinary, kidney, and digestive dis-eases; aids assimilation

Citrine–Rutilated

Color: Gold and metallic
Chakra: Solar plexus

- Steps up solar plexus energy to a higher level, increases energy and light

- Aids information assimilation, detoxifies and cleanses kundalini chakras and channels gently but completely
- Raises intellect, psychic ability and understanding of psychic information; keeps one in body while meditating and doing psychic work
- Increases self-awareness, promotes enlightenment, aids channeled writing

Cobaltite

Color: Dark pink
Chakra: Heart

- Brings light into the heart, fills heart scars with light to dissolve them, "lightens" heart pain and old traumas, relieves heart burdens
- Heals sadness and hurts, relieves those who carry others' pain with their own, helps bodhisattvas who suffer for others and the planet

Copper

Color: copper, metallic
Chakra: Hara chakra

- Grounds incoming spiritual energy into the hara chakra for storage and distribution
- Creates balanced use and assimilation of ch'i
- Grounds uncomfortable sensations and spaciness from too much psychic energy, reduces clairsentience, removes others' symptoms from one's energy
- Opens and heals the hara line chakras and the hara chakra itself
- Cleanses the emotional body of old negative emotions, offers emotional protection in crowds

Coral–Black

Color: Black
Chakra: Earth chakra

- Represents the Wiccan horned god, the male son-lover of the Goddess, male fertility, union with the Goddess, conception, and fatherhood
- Evokes the protector of the mother and child, protector of the family, and protector of the Goddess Earth
- Nurtures psychic masculinity, symbolizes the ritual high priest who bows to the priestess Goddess, supports the male who respects women and life

Coral–Blue

Color: Blue
Chakra: Throat

- Calms, stabilizes fear and insecurity
- Heals one's relationship with her inner child, facilitates inner-child work and healing
- Helps in understanding children, learning to be around children, and learning to play with children as an adult
- Supports expressing one's child self

Coral–Pink

Color: Pink or peach
Chakra: Heart

- Supports pregnancy, giving birth, and the new infant; eases morning sickness, eases fear of becoming a mother and fear of delivery

- Helps baby feel wanted and secure; helps baby adjust to a new incarnation; eases colic and crying, infant distress
- Alleviates mother's postpartum depression, aids nursing

*Coral–Red
☼

Color: Orange red
Chakra: Belly

- Aids conception and pregnancy, heals the ovaries and fallopian tubes, stimulates ovulation
- Draws baby's spirit to its karmically chosen mother's womb, may also be used to aid adoption process
- Eases childbirth, aids new mother's adjustment and bonding to her baby, aids new baby's entrance into incarnation
- Heals the adult's inner child, heals adults who were adopted children, helps in mother-daughter healing

Coral–Tampa Bay (Agate Fossilized)
☼

Color: Brown, orange, tan
Chakra: Belly

- Calms and balances overactive sexuality; grounds too-fast rise of kundalini, kundalini reactions
- Eases spaciness, dizziness; helps those having hallucinations, hearing voices, having frightening visions, feeling too much heat, or having creeping sensations
- Calms and soothes, brings understanding of what is wrong and how to ground it, grounds and centers

Coral–White

Color: White
Chakra: Crown

- Helps children adjust to being in new bodies, aids in their awareness of spirit guides and "invisible playmates"
- Stabilizes children's psychic abilities and protects them from being shut down by adults' criticism
- Aids growth of the physical body
- Supports optimal physical emotional and psychic development
- Protects vulnerability and innocence in children and adults

Crocoite

Color: Orange red
Chakra: Belly

- Fosters sexual healing, heals sexual difficulties or dysfunctions, helps those who are unable to sustain a sexual relationship
- Heals venereal dis-eases, sexual addictions and aberrations; heals the womb and emotions of too frequent abortions
- Helps those who have experienced incest, rape, or battering to accept a new and healthy sexual relationship and partner
- Aids return of hormonal balance after hysterectomy

Danburite

Color: Silver white
Chakra: Vision

- Intensifies, purifies, and magnifies all other healing energies; transforms negative energy and blocks into positivity and light

- Opens the galactic chakras; opens visual awareness of other realms, planets, and dimensions; increases psychic vision, and connection with mind grid and Light Body
- Increases connection with angels, guides, oversoul, positive extraterrestrial healers, and teachers; reinforces ability to perceive other levels of beyond-earthplane awareness
- Enhances creativity, mental awareness, awareness of the Void and Nonvoid
- Fosters gentle opening at user's pace

Diamond
✿

Color: Clear
Chakra: Transpersonal point

- Fills hara and kundalini line chakras and channels with light, connects with spirit guides and Goddess
- Merges karmic union marriage with soul's life purpose, anchors spiritual union into earthplane bodies
- Fulfills marriage contract made with mate in the pre-life state, holds the template of the marriage, promotes harmony, and balance in relationship and marriage

A diamond retains the karmic imprint of the marriage even after the relationship or life of the wearer ends.

Diopside
✿

Color: Green
Chakra: Heart

- Opens the higher intuition and higher mental body level, aids in the ability to honor one's intuition and follow its directions
- Fosters ability to feel and honor one's real thoughts, emotions, and feelings

- Opens the heart and mind to others, increases compassion for the suffering of others and oneself, opens the need to help others and the Earth
- Heals the heart, calms, improves blood circulation, lowers blood pressure, reduces stress

*Dioptase
—✶—

Color: Green
Chakra: Heart

- Releases past-life and this-life major emotional traumas
- Heals the inner child, opens and heals heart scars gently
- Calms, relieves physical and emotional pain, heals the physical body through healing the heart
- Releases past abuse, promotes karmic understanding, protects and returns lost vulnerability
- A happy, playful energy

This stone can self-destruct during intense healing; it is an expensive, very soft, very beautiful stone.

Dioptase–Malachite
—✶—

Color: Green and black
Chakra: Diaphragm

- Detoxifies traumas and heart pain from past lives for present life healing and release, heals negative karmic patterns about heart and relationship issues
- Opens and clears heart scars
- Brings karmic pain and patterns into conscious awareness for clearing, furthers lessons from past lives completed in this life, releases and heals karma

Dolomite

Color: Pink
Chakra: Heart

- Aids physical body calcium metabolism; aids osteoporosis, broken bones, tooth and jaw dis-ease
- Opens the heart to trust of self and Goddess, brings inner certainty, self-confidence, and positive self-love
- Calms; aids insomnia, nightmares, irregular sleep patterns; soothes night fears

Dumortierite

Color: Blue
Chakra: Throat

- Opens and balances the throat chakra; aids shyness, stage fright
- Develops ability to speak out; decreases self-effacement; aids in speaking for what one knows is real and true
- Fosters feeling secure, inner peace, and certainty
- Clears the throat and calms the mind; aids meditation and communication with spirit guides and angels; promotes reception of psychic communication from spirit guides, pets, other people

Eilat Stone

Color: Dark aqua
Chakra: Thymus

- Clears and opens the thymus chakra and balances it with the heart, detoxifies and releases soul-damaging traumas from this and past lives

;lears the Akashic records of old traumas specific to being abused as a woman—rape, incest, battering, misogyny, repression

- Heals women's lack of self-esteem and develops inner knowing
- Fosters pride in being a woman, encourages women's autonomy

*Emerald
※

Color: Green
Chakra: Diaphragm

- Heals the purged and cleansed diaphragm chakra and emotional body, reprograms the diaphragm chakra and emotional body/hara line
- Detoxifies negativity, transforms negativity into positive emotional energy
- Stabilizes; soothes; offers a sense of security, harmony, closeness to Goddess
- Increases understanding of one's life purpose in relation to the universal plan, aids in emotional and life stage transitions and changes

Epidote
※

Color: Green-black
Chakra: Diaphragm

- Causes purging and cathartic detoxification of negative emotions from the aura, cleanses held-onto and repressed emotions once and for all
- Opens those who have refused their spiritual growth and may not do it gently, drastically clears the emotional body aura

Those drawn to this stone are being shaken from resistance into rapid spiritual awakening.

Fluorite–Aqua

❖

Color: Aqua
Chakra: Throat

- Releases tears, aids expression of one's withheld grief and fear; aids the ability to ask others for help, healing, and comfort
- Fosters safe expression of anger, releases and heals anger, resolves fear
- Aids letting go of grief and emotional pain, releases the thought form that suffering is necessary in one's life

Fluorite–Blue

❖

Color: Blue
Chakra: Third eye

- Reprograms the mind and mental body, accesses information from the Akashic Records
- Releases negative karmic patterns, rewrites karma, offers knowledge of the past and past lives to heal their damage in the present, positively changes karma by healing the past and thereby reprogramming the present and future
- Offers access to the Lords of Karma, spirit guides, and angels; heals core soul fragmentation; stops negative thinking patterns

Fluorite–Clear

❖

Color: Clear, grey
Chakra: Vision

- Operates as a computer chip, in order to access the subconscious mind and the ninety percent of the brain that is unused; the brain as a computer; evokes information/light

- Provides access to the mental body grid, Earth grid, and interplanetary grid
- Supports telepathic contact with other people, discarnates, spirit guides, other-planetary Be-ings
- Facilitates communication with animals and other life forms
- Reprograms negative thought forms and patterns, heals subpersonalities, offers a psychic protection filter

*Fluorite–Gold
☼

Color: Gold, yellow
Chakra: Solar plexus

- Clears mental access to the Light Body, improves access to the mental grid
- Stimulates, clears, and heals all powers of the mind—the intellect, visualization, psychic ability, psychic healing, neurolinguistic programming, mental reprogramming, karmic release, idea and energy assimilation
- Aids uncording and removing of chakra hooks, clears attachments, heals subpersonalities and negative inner voices

Fluorite–Green
☼

Color: Green
Chakra: Heart

- Brings mental body/mind level changes and reprogramming into the emotional body and heart chakra
- Uses the mind to release emotional traumas from this lifetime
- Aids effectiveness of affirmations and mantras, aids visualization and meditation

- Heals heart scars, furthers emotional release, opens the heart to understanding what happened in the past, aids in integrating multiple personalities

Fluorite–Pink

Color: Pink
Chakra: Heart

- Reprograms the mind at the astral/emotional level, heals the astral body, helps to bring the astral self/astral twin into the body
- Aids soul retrieval's recovery of soul parts, heals soul fragmentation
- Aids emotional integration, soothes fear and despair, encourages forgiveness of self and others
- Accesses the Goddess within; engenders trust in life, self-love, self-empowerment, emotional wholeness
- Heals heart dis-eases, headaches, migraines

**Fluorite–Purple*

Color: Purple
Chakra: Crown

- Facilitates entrance into the programming of the mind at the spiritual level, accesses spiritual information from the Body of Light
- Makes spiritual knowledge from the outer aura body levels conscious
- Aids ability to meditate, increases psychic development, aids understanding oneself as a part of the universal plan, fosters wholeness and spiritual peace

Fossil

Color: Brown, grey, white
Chakra: Grounding

- Stimulates reading the ancient wisdom of the Earth, brings ancient Earth awareness and knowledge of the strength and ancient wisdom of the soul
- Gives access to root wisdom of peoples and the planet, Earth and soul origins
- Brings awareness of the soul's individual record on this planet and individual connection to the Earth
- Fosters respect for age, brings awareness that there is no death or end
- Promotes grounding, serenity, peaceful aging, inner strength, and endurance

Fuchsite

Color: Light green
Chakra: Diaphragm

- Collects emotions into the diaphragm chakra for opening and release, soothes the release process
- Aids nausea

This stone is not a strong healing energy.

*Garnet

Color: Red
Chakra: Root

- Opens root chakra; warms, grounds, and directs kundalini energy into the root center; draws Earth energy into the body

- Stimulates life force, causes acceptance and balances in the incarnation, boosts sexuality and fertility
- Repels disharmonious others from your aura energy—sometimes drastically and decisively; brings out anger and sexual attraction
- Draws your harmonious and sexually compatible mate to you, brings sexual healing
- Promotes tantric sex, promotes monogamous and stable marriage, aids in finding same or opposite sex true lovers

Gem Silica

Color: Aqua
Chakra: Thymus

- Clears the energies of sexual, emotional, and physical abuse from the emotional body
- Heals this-life and past-life traumas, prevents this-life traumas from becoming karmic patterns, heals past-life karmic patterns of abuse
- Connects with Goddess, brings self-empowerment
- Fosters joy in being a woman, aids women's all-healing

Goshenite (Clear Beryl)

Color: Clear
Chakra: Vision

- Aids ability to see and clear old patterns and pain
- Encourages karmic healing, brings about the visioning of past life traumas to release and heal them
- Reprograms karma through understanding past-life pain manifested in this lifetime, eases fear of karmic "seeing" and of reexperiencing the past

- Aids in understanding old patterns and filling in the missing pieces of information, completes karmic information and clearing
- Fills the soul with light and hope, fosters karmic grace

Halite (Salt)–Blue
※

Color: Blue
Chakra: Third eye

- Disinfects the third eye and all the kundalini chakras and channels of negative energy, attachments, entities, spirit possessions, and psychic attacks
- Removes negative influence from one's psychic perceptions and psychic senses, especially from clairvoyance
- Clears blocks to one's psychic opening, development, or abilities
- Heals distorted sense of reality on mental and psychic levels

This crystal draws negativity into itself and must be cleared frequently in sunlight (not water) to release it.

Halite (Salt)–Clear
※

Color: Clear, white
Chakra: Transpersonal point

- Disinfects the aura of negative energy, negative thought forms, entities, and attachments; repels and removes negativity
- Protects from negative entities, psychic attacks, possessions
- Aids in changing negative thought patterns and bad habits
- Protects those who use alcohol from bringing home bar attachments

Halite draws negativity into itself and must be cleared frequently in sunlight (not water) to release it.

Halite (Salt)–Pink

✦

Color: Pink, Lavender
Chakra: Crown

- Disinfects the crown and all the kundalini chakras and channels from negative energy, entities, spirit possessions, and attachments
- Repels and removes negativity from one's spiritual outlook, clears blocks to one's spiritual opening or development, clears blocks from one's psychic abilities
- Protects those who use alcohol from bringing home bar attachments

The crystal draws negativity into itself and must be cleared frequently in sunlight (not water) to release it.

Hawk's Eye

✦

Color: Black and silver
Chakra: Vision

- Works by increasing the psychic's ability to see what is wrong and then change it, transforms negative energy into positive, heals negative energy brought in from past lives
- Increases ability to see and release karmic attachments and negative entities from the aura, clears and grounds negative energy from the hara line, fosters ability to see and clear hara chakra hooks
- Increases night vision and psychic vision

*Hematite

✦

Color: Black over red
Chakra: Earth chakra

- Grounds and stabilizes one's incarnation into the earthplane
- Heals karmic anger and rage, heals those who were warriors in past lives and in this life, provides courage in facing karmic battles and courage in wartime or childbirth
- Supports facing and healing the shadow side of the self
- Fosters peace and nonaggression
- Stops bleeding and hemorrhaging, prevents excessive bleeding in childbirth, helps menstrual flooding

*Herkimer Diamond

✦

Color: Clear
Chakra: Transpersonal point

- Evokes pure love and pure information/light; stimulates gentle transformation; brings harmony within, with others, and with one's world
- Fine tunes aura energy and the etheric, emotional, mental and spiritual bodies; aligns physical and spiritual self
- Creates mental clarity, expands awareness and positivity, engenders the feeling of having everything one needs
- Supports living in the present peacefully, connects other dimensions and stars to one's life purpose and to the Earth
- Connects the individual to the universal grid, her Light Body, and oversoul; aids soul retrieval; draws one's soul mate and soul friends
- Fosters core soul healing, comforts

Heulandite

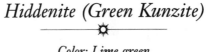

Color: White
Chakra: Third eye

- Programs the mental body for the ability to create one's own reality
- Brings about entrance into the Void—the creation/mental source of all existence
- Aids understanding that all limits are in the mind, heals the mind and releases limitation
- Furthers the ability to manifest a good life

Hiddenite (Green Kunzite)

Color: Lime green
Chakra: Diaphragm

- Detoxifies the physical body of emotional pain, heals dis-ease resulting from repressed emotions of this and past-life origin
- Aids one's ability to feel emotions, releases fear, promotes compassion for others and reaching out to others
- Increases self-awareness, discernment, letting go; fosters trust in Goddess

Hole-y Stone

Color: Brown
Chakra: Grounding

- Creates a psychic link with nature realms; look through the hole it permits viewing of fairies, devas, leprechauns, elves, sprites, pixies

- Gives a new view of the small lives of the Earth; develops compassion for and communication with animals, plants, insects, birds
- Increases respect and honor for the oneness of all life

Howlite

Color: White and grey
Chakra: Vision

- Creates and unmasks delusion and illusion in one's life, aids in creating and dissolving masks and costumes on the mental level
- Reveals self-delusion and the deluding of others
- Helps prevent tearing down reality or refusing one's truth to create a deception
- Expands consciousness, refuses limitation; can be used positively or as a negative escape for oneself, honestly or dishonestly toward others

Iolite (Water Sapphire)

Color: Indigo
Chakra: Third eye

- Opens, heightens, and expands psychic abilities in a gentle way; teaches the parameters of one's psychic abilities and possibilities
- Aids those of strong potential who are new on the spiritual path, encourages and protects psychic exploration
- Enhances curiosity and achievement, guides one through spiritual beginnings and growth

Ivory (or Bone)

❀

Color: White, beige
Chakra: Third eye

- Promotes recognition of the ancientness of the Earth, engenders respect for all species
- Encourages thanks for what the animals have given us to sustain and enhance human lives, brings awareness of extinct and endangered species and respect for the oneness of all life
- Encourages giving nuture and support to other people and animals and receiving it for oneself
- Promotes honoring the abundance and living beauty of the planet

Jade–Black

❀

Color: Black
Chakra: Earth chakra

- Aids in coming fully into incarnation for the purpose of enlightenment
- Aids understanding and healing karma, promotes ego nonattachment
- Fosters peace on Earth and in oneself, promotes Earth healing and environmental awareness
- Increases compassion for other-than-human lives on Earth (animals, plants, insects, birds)
- Facilitates communication with animals, engenders respect for the oneness of all life

*Jade–Green
※

Color: Dark green
Chakra: Heart

- Opens the qualities of mercy and compassion for all sentient Be-ings, inspires awareness of the oneness of all that lives
- Opens and heals the heart; frees one from anger, selfishness, and greed
- Encourages service to others and the planet
- Aids bodhisattvas and those on the path of enlightenment, stimulates Kwan Yin energy
- Soothes the emotions, heals the hips and kidneys, aids movement on one's life path
- Promotes trust in Goddess, fosters calm acceptance of the suffering in life, encourages giving to others

Jade–Pink
※

Color: Pink, peach
Chakra: Heart

- Opens one's heart to all sentient be-ings including oneself, increases compassion for the suffering of all life
- Aids those who take the Bodhisattva Vow, supports bodhisattvas incarnated on Earth, aids all those in service to others and the planet
- Heals the heart, aids healers' burnout and despair

Jade–Yellow
※

Color: Yellow
Chakra: Solar plexus

- Helps those on the Buddhist path to enlightenment or other spiritual paths; aids meditation, visualization, and

learning nonattachment; helps overcome ego, selfishness, and greed
- Stimulates and heals the mental body, heightens awareness and compassion
- Helps understand that enlightenment happens only through incarnation
- Fosters respect for the body; promotes a peaceful mind; soothes digestive and urinary systems

Jasper–Brown
✺

Color: Brown and orange
Chakra: Hara chakra

- Protects and repairs the energy envelope of the etheric double aura; heals aura tears from trauma, anesthetics, prescription or recreational drugs, alcohol use, fear, physical pain, or psychic attack
- Helps to retain aura integrity against negative energy and others' negative thought forms, helps filter out the negative mass consciousness
- Helps delineate boundaries between self and others

Jasper–Leopard Skin
✺

Color: Brown and orange
Chakra: Hara chakra

- Opens conscious knowledge of the living library, encodes the herstory of all peoples that came to colonize Earth and the planets they came from
- Encodes the herstory and origins of all species brought to Earth and developed here, and the herstory of life on Earth since other-planetary arrival

- Contains the keys to the future development of Earth peoples and species, helps manifest twelve-strand DNA healing
- Protects those who work with the living library, increases information/light

Jasper–Leopard Skin
✪

Color: Brown and tan
Chakra: Grounding

- Offers protection as one manifests one's path, protects one while fulfilling one's life purpose and karmic agreements on the earthplane
- Offers help along the path, increases safety and security in achieving life goals
- Grounds into daily life and daily work, helps to turn one's life work into one's daily occupation or job, aids concentration and ability to focus

Jasper–Picture
✪

Color: Green, grey, tan
Chakra: Vision

- Stimulates visualization of this-life and past-life scenes, evokes visions from lifetimes on other planets
- Promotes awareness of the beauty of the Earth
- Aids ability to visualize and meditate, stabilizes creativity, brings new ideas for visual artists, opens artists' blocks, aids drawing and painting

*Jasper–Red

Color: Red orange
Chakra: Belly

- Balances anger and sexuality, heals women's anger at men, calms men's sexual aggressiveness toward women
- Helps balance sexuality with feeling in gay and heterosexual relationships, promotes sexual compatibility between lovers, inspires tantric sex
- Balances irregular menstrual cycles, aids ovulation, alleviates menstrual cramps, brings on menstruation

Jasper–Yellow

Color: Yellow-tan
Chakra: Movement

- Protects and repairs the etheric double aura from the groin area down: thighs, legs, knees, feet
- Protects those whose movement on their life path is vulnerable to distraction and scattering, aids those who are accident prone or clumsy

This stone is not a strong healing energy but is useful for some people, especially children.
For other jaspers, also see Bloodstone, Mugglestone, and Wonderstone.

Jet

Color: Black
Chakra: Earth chakra

- Heals the grief of losing one's place among the stars, heals longing for the soul's home

- Helps to accept the limits of incarnation and the body, helps to accept the Earth as where one needs to be for the present
- Opens ancient wisdom, the souls' wisdom, the wisdom of the body, and the wisdom of the planet

Kunzite–Clear

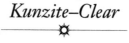

Color: Clear
Chakra: Transpersonal point

- Heals core soul damage and damage from past lives, reunites fragmented soul parts
- Aids soul retrieval and emotional body healing, aligns and balances energy
- Promotes astral healing, brings astral twin self into physical aura, resolves karma

**Kunzite–Green*

See Hiddenite.

Kunzite–Pink

Color: Pink, lavender
Chakra: Heart

- Calms, balances, stabilizes; brings peace, compassion; increases ability to open the heart to trust and love
- Protects vulnerability, heals negativity in oneself and negativity received from others caused by fear and insecurity
- Connects and clears the heart, throat, third eye, and crown; opens blocks in the kundalini chakras caused by self-protection due to past emotional pain and trauma

- Opens the heart's ability to give, forgive, and receive; heals emotions and the emotional body
- Aids working with spirit guides for healing and self-healing, fosters trust in Goddess and oneself

Kyanite–Aqua

Color: Aqua
Chakra: Thymus

- Opens, clears, and balances the thymus chakra, connects the emotional body/hara line to the etheric body/kundalini line
- Enables one to process feelings and release sorrow, alienation, anger, and grief
- Encourages compassion for the suffering and oneness of all life; fosters compassion for oneself, forgiveness, and self-forgiveness
- Increases the ability to reach out to others and to love again after loss

Kyanite–Black

Color: Black
Chakra: Earth chakra

- Roots the current incarnation into the earthplane, opens and balances the hara line chakras and channels
- Opens one's intergalactic and interplanetary heritage as an Earth Be-ing in this Earth changes lifetime
- Brings awareness of Earth stewardship, aids contact with other-planetary help and helpers
- Fosters understanding of the immortality of the soul and the between-life state

- Aids meditation, past-life regression work, future-life progression, and meditation between lives; grounds, calms, and centers

*Kyanite–Blue
❖

Color: Silver blue
Chakra: Causal body

- Connects kundalini and hara line channels at the thymus; balances, aligns, opens, expands, and heals kundalini and hara energy channels and chakras
- Heals blockages and burnout from all aura bodies—etheric, emotional, mental, and spiritual
- Heals throat dis-eases and blockages, aids communication physically and psychically
- Develops telepathy-empathy with spirit guides, angels, discarnate Be-ings, pets, and extraterrestrials
- Aids manifesting one's life work on the earthplane
- Boosts immune system

Kyanite–Brown
❖

Color: Orange brown
Chakra: Hara chakra

- Opens and expands the hara chakra and entire hara line, balances energy
- Stabilizes and aids one's life purpose, helps one to understand and manifest one's life purpose and life agreements on the earthplane
- Stimulates and increases the Ch'i Kung microcosmic orbit, boosts and stabilizes the life force, is all-balancing and all-healing

Kyanite with Rubellite

❋

Color: Blue and red-violet
Chakra: Causal body

- Opens and balances the causal body chakra, opens and balances all the hara line chakras and channels
- Brings spiritual and soul level information to bear upon one's life purpose and path
- Manifests one's life purpose on the earthplane, increases calmness and confidence in one's life and life work, encourages certainty of the way
- Spiritualizes one's life, repairs twelve-strand DNA, aids those on the bodhisattva path

This important, newly available gemstone energy helps us regain our full potential, as the hara line is central to current human development.

Labradorite–Golden

❋

Color: Yellow, gold
Chakra: Solar plexus

- Heals the will, aids concentration, promotes courage and clarity
- Helps one to take one's freedom, heals those who subject themselves to others' manipulation and those who manipulate others, heals codependency, co-alcoholism
- Fills the etheric double, emotional body aura, and mental body aura with light; opens and heals the mental body and Body of Light
- Connects with the mental grid and Earth grid, heals confusion and indecision

*Labradorite–Grey

❁

Color: Silver grey
Chakra: Vision

- Connects the emotional and mental bodies to one's life purpose and physical action, activates the hara line
- Protects and clears the aura of negative energy, psychic attacks, negative alien interference and implants, attachments, and spirit possessions
- Opens eye/vision chakras for using the eyes as lasers in psychic healing
- Opens the ability for accurate pendulum use, increases psychic vision and visualization
- Aids the ability to see and communicate with positive other-planetary Be-ings and protects from negative ones
- Connects one to the light grid and galactic healing levels
- Fosters consciousness of life purpose, provides a transformative and intense energy

Lake Michigan Concretion

❁

Color: Brown
Chakra: Grounding

- Brings rootedness into the Earth, evokes a reminder of Goddess as the Earth herself, helps one know the Goddess's support and nurturing
- Increases awareness of having everything one needs for an abundant life, enhances security and safety
- Contributes to knowing oneself as taken care of on the Goddess Earth
- Increases fertility and creativity, grounds

This stone is a natural Goddess image of ancient type.

*Lapis Lazuli

Color: Blue
Chakra: Throat and third eye

- Cleanses the mental body, promotes deep penetration to heal outdated thought forms and mental patterns
- Prevents negative thoughts from becoming karmic patterns, releases outworn karmic patterns for healing
- Changes negative views of reality to positive outlooks, heals mental body damage from old traumas in this life, reprograms the mental body, facilitates all healing

Lapis is best worn with other stones like Amethyst or Rose Quartz to mellow and gentle its effects.

*Larimar

Color: Blue and white
Chakra: Throat

- Helps soul mates to find and recognize each other, heals negative karma between soul mates and lovers
- Opens honest communication between soul mates, fosters speaking and listening with awareness and putting the other and the relationship first
- Stabilizes new relationships between soul mates
- Inspires calm certainty, opens creativity and the throat

*Lepidolite

Color: Lavender, pink
Chakra: Crown

- Connects heart and crown to bring spiritual understanding to suffering and pain; brings understanding of the growth brought by, and the purpose of, heart pain

- Brings understanding of one's life purpose and place in the universal plan
- Opens and releases pain and suffering layer by layer, releases karmic suffering—the "Cross of St. Michael"
- Brings acceptance, calm, trust in life and the Goddess; heals fear at its source in this or past lifetimes

Lepidolite with Mica
☼

Color: Red violet
Chakra: Causal body

- Opens and develops the causal body chakra and spiritual body, stabilizes soul growth
- Balances psychic communication with earthplane daily functioning, brings spiritual information into daily life
- Aids channeling and mediumship, helps bring contact with spirit guides and angels

Also see Mica.

Lepidolite—Yellow
☼

Color: Yellow
Chakra: Solar plexus

- Calms fear; releases fears one at a time for viewing and releasing; opens and clears old, outmoded fears
- Releases psychic attacks, protects against psychic draining
- Dissolves cords and hooks from the solar plexus chakra only, protects and shields the solar plexus from incoming negative energy, acts as a chakra shield for the solar plexus

Also see Kyanite with Lepidolite.

Lodestone

Color: Brown metallic
Chakra: Grounding

- Protects the aura from negative energy and psychic attacks, clears negative energy from the aura by magnetics, balances aura energy and the acupuncture meridians
- Repels negativity back to its sender, creates a shield against harmful vibrations but lets positive energy through

Lodestone is usually self-clearing and is used in pairs.

Magnetite

Color: Brown metallic
Chakra: Grounding

- Balances energy polarities and acupuncture meridians, opens blocked acupuncture points, aids movement of ch'i/energy from the root chakra through the knees and feet
- Promotes grounding and ballast into the Earth, balances hara and kundalini line energy channels
- Maintains balance through life and along one's chosen path

*Malachite

Color: Green and black
Chakra: Diaphragm

- Detoxifies the emotional body, releases negative/painful emotions, clears and releases old traumas from this life and past lives
- Detoxifies liver and gall bladder at physical and emotional levels, brings things out from within

- Aids childbirth labor, aids emotional therapy and recovery process
- Protects against psychic attack and others' negativity, protects against poisoning

Malachite's deep energy cleansing may not be comfortable; use in small doses.

Marcasite

Color: Silver
Chakra: Vision

- Expands psychic vision, promotes clairvoyance, increases the ability to see discarnate entities and "ghosts"
- Protects and aids psychics who pass-over discarnate entities and de-haunt houses; aids in removal of spirit attachments, possessions, and entities in healing work and protects healers who do this work
- Protects from negative entities and energy

Mariposite

Color: Green and white
Chakra: Heart

- Reduces stress, calms and stabilizes, reduces fear, reduces energy overwhelm, lessens exhaustion
- Aids deeper breathing, helps attain calming breath
- Speeds regeneration and recovery, eases physical pain
- Functions as a mineral rescue remedy (all-healing)

Meteorite

Color: Metallic
Chakra: Galactic chakras

- Brings a message from the stars that we on Earth are neither alone nor abandoned by the universe, promises that the quarantine of planet Earth will end and a time of hope and peace will come
- Brings aid from high level Be-ings from other planets and dimensions
- Contacts other-planetary helpers and protects from negative alien energy

Mica

Color: Silver
Chakra: Vision

- Aids in perceiving the eyes as the windows of the soul, develops the vision chakras as reflectors of soul level growth and development
- Helps to understand the levels and layers of soul structure and the between-life state
- Improves psychic ability to visualize, increases ability to see the many layers of a situation from a spiritual perspective and to discern reality and illusion

Also see Lepidolite with Mica.

Mica–Muscovite

Color: Silver
Chakra: Vision

- Sorts out and puts in perspective one's thoughts, problems, and priorities; establishes a one-thing-at-a-time order

- Takes problems and processes them step-by-step for working them out more easily; breaks large problems and projects into smaller, easy steps
- Aids concentration and focus, aids in completion of what one starts
- Reduces stress, promotes living in the present

*Moldavite
❖

Color: Dark green
Chakra: Movement

- Connects to positive Pleiadian helpers and healers for protection, encourages healing and self-healing
- Removes negative past-life alien implants; protects from negative alien interference; removes spirit attachments, entities, and spirit possessions
- Offers good protection for Earth healers and psychics who remove implants and attachments from others
- Gives freedom to move among the dimensions and planets while remaining safe on Earth, acts as a psychic opener and enhancer
- Fosters other-planetary contact through dreams and meditation, protects astral travel

Moonstone–Blue
❖

Color: Light blue
Chakra: Throat

- Focuses one on the psychic abilities of empathy and telepathy, sending and receiving
- Helps to communicate psychically with people, pets, discarnate entities, plant or animal devas, Goddesses, spirit guides, and angels—Be-ings in or out of body

- Aids communication with other-planetary Be-ings; aids communication across time, dimension, space, and the galaxy; aids psychic hearing
- Helps to honor oneself as a psychic Be-ing and a part of Goddess, encourages self-blessing, and psychic healing

Moonstone–Grey

Color: Silver grey
Chakra: Vision

- Focuses one on the psychic abilities of vision and clairvoyance, psychic sight and knowing
- Creates new realities and understanding other than earth-plane realities
- Aids visualization, meditation, guided journeys, shamanic journeys, visual psychic healing
- Helps one to see extraterrestrials, discarnate entities, spirit guides, angels, Goddesses, and devas
- Expands one's spiritual and psychic vision, helps to see oneself as a part of Goddess and the universal plan
- Increases ability to focus on one's life path

Moonstone–Peach

Color: Peach, pink
Chakra: Heart

- Heals the heart by bringing the Goddess/love into it, fosters spiritual and psychic opening through heart and emotional healing
- Helps to discover women's and one's own place in the universal plan, helps to discover oneself as Goddess within

- Gently clears heart scars and traumas from this and past lives, aids in easing self-criticism and learning to be gentle with oneself, fosters acceptance and openness
- Aids in learning to trust the Goddess and oneself and in learning to honor oneself as a woman, manifests women's all-healing

*Moonstone–White
✺

Color: White
Chakra: Third eye

- Supports women's connection to the Goddess and the moon
- Regulates menstrual and fertility cycles, menopause
- Enhances psychic "lunar" knowing, psychic sight, entrance into other-than-earthplane realities
- Increases intuition, advances ancient women's wisdom, helps develop magick and the Craft, enhances ritual
- Soothes and heals the emotions and mind, aids spiritual growth and development, heals the astral body

Morganite (Pink Beryl)
✺

Color: Pink
Chakra: Causal body

- Opens causal body chakra for transmission of spiritual level healing to the emotional body
- Raises energy vibration of emotional and astral levels, heals astral body and emotional heart
- Heals and returns fragmented soul parts, aids soul retrieval, aligns astral and etheric bodies
- Heals karmic emotional pain, eases chronic karmic suffering and pain from past-life traumas

Mother-of-Pearl
❖

Color: White
Chakra: Third eye

- Soothes, reduces stress and worry, increases knowledge that everything is okay
- Helps to see a positive reality, heals friction in one's life, helps one learn to flow with life
- Engenders a sense of safety and security, brings emotional shelter
- Balances physical energy, provides lymphatic and immune support, puts one in touch with the all-nurturing Mother Goddess

Mugglestone (Hematite and Jasper)
❖

Color: Black and tan
Chakra: Grounding

- Focuses one's energy on the body and the earthplane; grounds, centers, balances
- Protects the integrity of the etheric double aura from tears and rips, repairs the damaged aura envelope, protects against and repels psychic attacks
- Gathers and calms scattered energies, reduces stress particularly when induced by conflicts with other people
- Aids recovery from anesthetics and surgeries, reduces bleeding

*Obsidian–Black

Color: Black
Chakra: Earth chakra

- Promotes grounding into one's Earth's origins and the soul's origins on other planets, opens awareness of past lives, reveals awareness of negative karma to clear and heal it
- Increases awareness of the body and centering of the soul into incarnation, grounds spirit into body after psychic work
- Stabilizes fear and panic states, grounds and centers

This is a good stone for scrying and for past-life regression.

Obsidian–Mahogany

Color: Brown and black
Chakra: Earth

- Roots one's life purpose into that of healing the planet; promotes Earth stewardship, activism, environmentalism
- Helps psychic healers who focus on Earth healing and helps activists against species extinction
- Aids those who care for animals, reptiles, birds, insects, and plants or the land and seas
- Supports and prevents burnout and discouragement, aids communication with nonhuman species and nature devas

Obsidian–Purple Sheen

Color: Black
Chakra: Earth chakra

- Connects with the Lords of Karma, heals one's past life and current karma in this lifetime, heals the past to heal the present and future

- Promotes rewriting one's Akashic Records, aids past-life regression and future-life progression
- Aids in understanding one's present lifetime in terms of what has gone before—and heals the difficulties permanently, both karmic patterns and negative karma

Obsidian–Rainbow
❈

Color: Black
Chakra: Earth chakra

- Aids in bringing soul awareness into the body, spiritualizes the incarnation for greater soul growth
- Brings karmic healing, creates an understanding of how past lives have created present-life situations, heals karmic patterns and releases the damage of the past
- Helps attain enlightenment in this lifetime, enhances work with the Lords of Karma, aids in becoming an old soul

Obsidian–Snowflake
❈

Color: Black and white
Chakra: Earth chakra

- Opens awareness of past lives and of having had many incarnations; increases knowledge that we have been here before and will be here again, that there is no death of the soul
- Aids in past-life meditation and regression work, and in understanding the present in terms of the past, heals karma and karmic patterns

Okenite

Color: White
Chakra: Galactic chakras

- Opens and clears the Light Body for connection to the mind grid, Earth grid, and intergalactic grid
- Makes one a channel for other-planetary aid to Earth, extends one's perception beyond Earth and into the stars, opens and clears Earthly limitations of being bound to the planet or the body
- Transforms limitations and karma

Okenite is good for star people serving on Earth. This stone is not of Earthly origin.

Onyx–Black

Color: Black
Chakra: Earth

- Reinforces the knowledge that there is no death; aids understanding the wheel of birth, death, and rebirth
- Brings about the knowledge that separation is an illusion and reunion will come
- Aids psychic contact with those who have died, facilitates seances and mediumship, brings messages from the dead, aids past-life and between-lives regression work
- Helps future life progressions, prevents and removes spirit possessions

Onyx-Green

☼

Color: Dark green
Chakra: Movement

- Heals karma obstructing progress on one's life path, clears the path to growth and movement
- Fosters achievement, manifests spiritual growth on the earthplane
- Heals confusion or resistance to one's life agreements, creates forward progress, supports painful knees

Onyx–Mexican White

☼

Color: White, tan, green
Chakra: Movement

- Promotes stability and steadfastness, eases immovability where refusal to move or change is positive
- Breaks pattern of immovability when change is needed and required

This stone is not a strong healing energy but is useful for a few people, mostly men.

Opal–Blue

☼

Color: Blue, grey, white
Chakra: Throat

- Intensifies the need and ability to express emotions and creativity, enhances expression of repressed emotions
- Opens communication between people, people and pets, people and spirit guides; aids psychic hearing, sending and receiving; promotes empathy and telepathy
- Soothes the throat, opens the voice, calms

Opal–Mexican Fire

Color: Orange and white
Chakra: Belly

- Lights the fires of positive sexuality, aids sexual healing
- Opens the pictures held in the belly chakra; releases and heals memories of incest, rape, and sexual abuse
- Aids in leaving battered or abusive relationships, helps to establish new relationships after trauma
- Encourages healthy sexuality and healthy sexual relationships (gay or heterosexual), stimulates orgasm

Opal–Oregon

Color: White
Chakra: Transpersonal point

- Heals and releases past emotional traumas from this and past lives
- Gently cleanses and heals emotional body and etheric double aura envelope
- Develops nurturing and self-nurturing, brings about release and relief
- Returns and heals lost soul fragments in soul retrieval process, protects soul fragments during healing
- Inspires imagination, childlike vulnerability, joyful rediscovery of self, positivity, and peace

Opal–White

Color: White
Chakra: Crown

- Opens and amplifies the energy of all the kundalini chakras, fills the kundalini line with color and light

- Amplifies negative patterns and behaviors for the purpose of clearing and releasing them
- Raises the kundalini, increases light and spiritual awareness, enhances spiritual initiation

Use with Rose Quartz for positivity and balance.

Peacock Ore

Color: Metallic blue, colors
Chakra: Third eye

- Opens the third eye/brow chakra; stimulates psychic opening, psychic vision, and clairvoyance
- Facilitates inner knowing, increases self-confidence on one's path, reinforces certainty of what one psychically sees
- Aids psychics learning to trust their abilities, helps with distance healing
- Helps in creating one's own reality, and manifesting by visualization

Pearl

Color: White
Chakra: Crown

- Soothes and heals the negativity and struggle in one's life
- Surrounds negative energy with light, dissolves negative energy, heals negative thoughts and thought forms
- Moves attachments and psychic attacks out of the aura, helps to release negative karmic patterns, fills the aura with healing light
- Calms and soothes the emotions, heals the negative inner voice and subpersonalities

Pecos Diamond (Pecos Quartz)

―❖―

Color: Orange
Chakra: Belly

- Transforms and transmutes anger; changes this-life and past-life anger and rage to understanding
- Encourages forgiveness and self-forgiveness; helps heal past sexual abuse, emotional abuse, rape, battering; releases karmic patterns of abuse from the aura
- Heals the inner child
- Helps to release chakra cords from all the kundalini chakras, protects clairsentient healers who take on others' symptoms, releases matching pictures between healer and receiver
- Expands compassion for others and oneself

*Peridot

―❖―

Color: Yellow green
Chakra: Diaphragm

- Balances the process of emotional release and healing, regulates detoxification of emotions to comfortable levels
- Heals emotional and physical pain, lightens suffering
- Fosters emotional balance, security, and inner peace
- Aids physical detoxification and helps the assimilation organs—liver, kidneys, bladder, gall bladder, stomach; heals ulcers, irritable bowel syndrome, kidney infections

Petrified Wood

※

Color: tan and green
Chakra: Movement

- Aids concentration, grounds, and centers those unable to persevere on their life path and life goals
- Slows one down; heals being scattered, flighty, and indecisive
- Helps those who cannot complete what they start, promotes setting and keeping goals, steadies and stabilizes
- Helps the spirit function in the body

Phenacite

※

Color: White, clear
Chakra: Transpersonal point

- Activates the hara line/emotional body; brings Heavenly Ch'i/Goddess energy into hara and kundalini chakras, channels, and meridians
- Fills the aura electrical system with light/information; increases light flow through the aura, chakras, and channels
- Balances energy, comforts, and stabilizes
- Aligns the aura bodies, facilitates core soul healing, manifests twelve-strand DNA, heals traumas and damage to the aura field on all body levels
- Offers energy protection, enhances a sense of oneself as part of a greater Goddess plan

Picasso Stone

Color: Black and brown
Chakra: Earth chakra

- Opens the galactic chakras for contact with positive other-planetary Be-ings as it grounds one to Earth
- Fosters contact with other-planetary Earth guardians and Earth healers, acts as a spaceship receiver
- Aids psychics who do Earth healing, shields against negative aliens and entities, aids star people incarnated in Earth bodies
- Supports channeling, intuition, creativity, inspiration

Pipestone

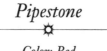

Color: Red
Chakra: Root

- Invokes the blood of the ancestors of Minnesota Native people, Native American heritage, the suffering of the people, survival of the people and traditions
- Represents the Great Mystery of all life (Buddhist Void, Wiccan Goddess), life itself, the sacredness and oneness of all life

This stone is sacred to Native Americans and is not for mundane or profane use. It is made into bowls for sacred ritual smoking pipes.

Pumice

Color: Pink
Chakra: Heart

- Helps to open the heart and get beyond old pain and defenses, especially for those whose abrasiveness creates difficulty in their lives

- Promotes gentleness and vulnerability, increases ability to give to others and to let others be close
- Encourages emotional healing, aids recovery, fosters ability to trust
- Helps old emotional wounds heal by letting the light in

Pyrite

Color: Metallic gold
Chakra: Solar plexus

- Assimilates and manifests higher-level energy, stabilizes energy levels and intake
- Receives expanded amounts of energy/light without becoming scattered or stressed
- Brings about optimal use of psychic energy, calms
- Aids prosperity and ability to manifest earthplane needs and abundance, uplifts and grounds at once

Pyromorphite

Color: Black, multi
Chakra: Earth chakra

- Fosters a soul connection to all life forms on the Earth, compassion for all Be-ings on the planet
- Aids psychic communication with plant and mineral devas, nature spirits, insects, trees, animals
- Induces awareness that all life is one life and what harms one harms all
- Fosters stewardship of the Earth and Earth healing

Quartz–Blue (Siderite)

❁

Color: Blue
Chakra: Third eye

- Opens and stimulates the third eye chakra to psychic ability and spirituality
- Increases telepathy and clairvoyance, aids psychic healing, brings contact with spirit guides and angels, promotes psychic vision
- Helps to see the world in a spiritual rather than earthplane way, switches earthplane illusion to spiritual reality, stabilizes new psychics

Quartz–Chlorite Inclusion

❁

Color: Green and clear
Chakra: Diaphragm

- Detoxifies the kundalini and hara lines; clears toxins absorbed from chemicals, petroleum, and pesticides from body tissues and all aura levels
- Clears environmental pollutants from the aura and physical body; processes air and water pollution, helps those with environmental illness, chronic fatigue, cancer, asthma, and liver damage

*Quartz–Clear Crystal

❁

Color: Clear
Chakra: Transpersonal point

- Fills the aura, chakras, and aura bodies with light; heals and aligns the etheric and emotional bodies
- Clears negativity at all levels, protects from negative energy, detoxifies the aura

- Promotes and intensifies spiritual expansion and awareness, promotes enlightenment
- Aids emotional stability, helps all physical and emotional dis-eases, speeds healing, brings goodness on every level

*Quartz–Elestial or Skeletal
※

Color: Brown or grey
Chakra: Grounding

- Aids in transformation, transition and change; encourages soul growth
- Grounds one into one's life path, sets one on the path, shows one "where one is going" and how to begin getting there
- Can cause sudden and drastic aura and life path shifts, provides karmic correction to straying from one's path, helps with fulfillment of karmic agreements and life purpose
- Produces deep release

Quartz–Fire (Lepidochrosite Inclusion)
※

Color: Deep pink
Chakra: Heart

- Opens the heart chakra and emotional body for major transformations and healing, opens the closed heart, prepares for deep psychic healing and karmic change
- Exposes and heals blocked past traumas from past lives and this life, removes past-life barriers to heart healing in this lifetime
- Helps incest survivors and survivors of rape and battering
- Aids in becoming whole hearted

Quartz–Green (Prase)

✳

Color: Light green
Chakra: Heart

- Soothes, calms, and refills the heart after emotional release; repairs the chakra after heart scar opening
- Manifests Kwan Yin energy of compassion and universal love, encourages love for self and others
- Heals abandonment, loneliness, and emotional upset
- Aids heart and emotional body healing, eases fear and panic attacks

Quartz–Grey Phantom

✳

Color: Grey, clear
Chakra: Vision

- Releases past-life information in visual flashbacks, moving rapidly from recent this-life scenes to older and older this-life scenes, then into past-life scenes
- Aids past-life regression and helps with work to release karmic issues and patterns

Use this stone briefly, then stop to process or ask to focus on a specific lifetime or pattern/problem to release.

Quartz–Lordite Inclusion

✳

Color: Red, grey, brown
Chakra: Causal body

- Clears interference in psychic transmission; aids in channeling, and psychic healing
- Helps with the "gutted fish" feeling after receiving major energy work

- Balances energy shifts in the aura, brings energy changes in the aura onto the physical level
- Strengthens contact with spirit guides, the Lords of Karma, ascended healers, and teachers; calms and stabilizes

Quartz–Moroccan Druzy
☼

Color: rose red
Chakra: Perineum

- Pulls energy downward through the hara line and into the perineum chakra and root chakra, connects perineum chakra and root chakra—the hara and kundalini lines; grounds the kundalini
- Acts as a sexual stimulant, a life force stimulant, and an energy stimulant
- Heals exhaustion, low vitality, chronic fatigue

Quartz–Red
☼

Color: Red brown
Chakra: Hara chakra

- Calms and grounds kundalini energy into the hara chakra, connects kundalini and hara channels, aids in opening hara line chakras and balancing kundalini chakras
- Balances earthplane and spiritual energy and focus, facilitates living as a spiritual Be-ing while incarnated in a body
- Aids blood circulation dis-eases, strengthens red blood cells

Quartz–Red Phantom

☼

Color: Orange and clear
Chakra: Belly

- Opens and releases memories, feelings and pictures of past this-life traumas and emotional pain
- Heals and releases anger, rage, resentment, terror, fear, and confusion
- Aids in the recovery process of sexual abuse survivors and those abandoned or abused as children
- Heals the hurt inner child by awakening one's ability to feel and process what had to be blocked to survive, heals the emotional body

Use in small doses.

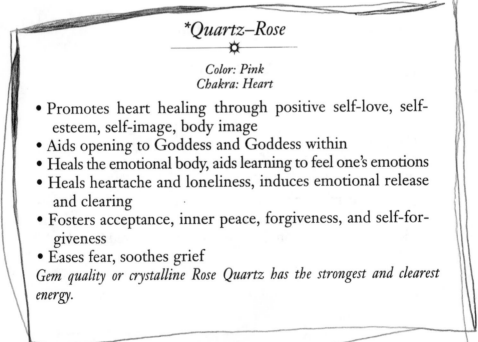

*Quartz–Rose

☼

Color: Pink
Chakra: Heart

- Promotes heart healing through positive self-love, self-esteem, self-image, body image
- Aids opening to Goddess and Goddess within
- Heals the emotional body, aids learning to feel one's emotions
- Heals heartache and loneliness, induces emotional release and clearing
- Fosters acceptance, inner peace, forgiveness, and self-forgiveness
- Eases fear, soothes grief

Gem quality or crystalline Rose Quartz has the strongest and clearest energy.

*Quartz–Rutilated

Color: Clear, gold
Chakra: Transpersonal point

- Expands the transmission of light/information entering the aura bodies, clears and expands the hara and kundalini channels and chakras
- Magnifies all positive energy entering the aura system, dispels all negative energy and energy blockages
- Speeds opening and releasing, intensifies

*Quartz–Smoky

Color: Black, brown
Chakra: Grounding

- Aids grounding into incarnation, creates acceptance of the body and the earthplane
- Stabilizes, enhances security and safety
- Promotes walking softly on the Earth Mother, encourages Earth awareness and responsibility
- Accepts one's place on the planet; heals fear, depression, addictions, obsessions

Quartz–Snow

Color: White
Chakra: Third eye

- Calms and balances the third eye chakra
- Helps those who fear their opening psychic abilities, teaches how to use new psychic abilities
- Aids learning to meditate, balances kundalini reactions, facilitates gentle opening

Quartz–Strawberry

Color: Pink and black
Chakra: Heart

- Creates balanced unconditional love for others and oneself, supports giving and receiving
- Aids in viewing life with understanding and compassion for all
- Fosters understanding of one's past lives as they have influenced this lifetime and understanding this lifetime's place in one's record of many lifetimes and incarnations
- Opens the heart while grounding one into this lifetime and body
- Creates compassion for the not-perfect body

Quartz–Tourmaline

Color: Black and clear
Chakra: Earth

- Protects one's life purpose for this incarnation, aids grounding one's life purpose into earthplane reality and manifesting it on the earthplane
- Aids in keeping one's agreed-upon pre-life, karmic contracts and reinforces remembering the reasons for one's current incarnation
- Helps one honor one's promises, life agreements, and path

Quartz–White Phantom

Color: White
Chakra: Transpersonal point

- Use in pairs for psychic surgery or paired with Black Velvet Tourmaline to balance Earth and Heavenly Ch'i and entire hara line
- Opens the galactic chakras beyond the transpersonal point; expands awareness into the Body of light, mind grid, and planetary grid
- Opens the aura to the positive aid of other-planetary healers, spirit guides, angels, Goddess
- Balances energy flow through the kundalini line, hara line, and all the chakras
- Expands the aura's ability to hold light/information/energy/ch'i

*Rhodochrosite

Color: Pink and yellow
Chakra: Heart

- Cleanses the heart chakra and emotional body of the need to suffer
- Releases karmic guilt as "the Cross of St. Michael," releases suffering from past lives held in the present-life aura
- Reprograms the emotional body to receive joy, heals the ability to give and receive
- Heals chronic self-blame, detoxifies physically and emotionally, heals digestive problems, and ulcers

Rhodochrosite–Gem Crystalline

Color: Peach, red
Chakra: Causal body

- Heals blocks to spiritual level energy entering the hara line
- Opens blocked ability to know and manifest one's life purpose and karmic agreements for this incarnation
- Heals lack of connection with Goddess, heals lack of spirituality in one's life, and lack of reason for Be-ing
- Prevents the emotional sources of cancer from manifesting, aids those who are dying because they have refused to keep their contracts for this lifetime

Rhodonite

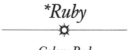

Color: Pink and black
Chakra: Heart

- Grounds emotional flights into earthplane reality
- Helps in recognizing real from wishful in relationships (for those who fall in love too fast and too often)
- Aids in seeing one's current flame as a real person
- Promotes maturity in love affairs and relationships, aids in distinguishing real from fantasy in love

**Ruby*

Color: Red
Chakra: Root and Perineum

- Intensifies life force energy in the root chakra and kundalini line
- Connects kundalini and hara lines at the perineum, thereby connecting life force with life purpose at the physical level

- Stimulates the will to live and the body's ability to support the incarnation
- Alleviates physical coldness, weakness, chronic blood diseases, chronic fatigue, low vitality

Ruby–Star
※

Color: Red violet
Chakra: Causal body

- Brings information/light into conscious awareness
- Aids contact with spirit guides, angels, positive extraterrestrials, other-dimensional Be-ings, and Goddesses
- Fosters channeling and automatic writing of other-level information, draws out information from and connection to the mind grid and Earth grid
- Aids in psychics who spend too much time out of body, stabilizes all levels
- Aids in chronic fatigue, weakness, and debility

Salmonite
※

Color: Tan, beige
Chakra: Movement

- Clears energy blockages in the knees by healing one's ability to move forward in life and on one's life path
- Aids those who resist or fear their agreed-upon life purpose
- Heals rigidity and inflexibility on the emotional level
- Aids dis-eases of the feet, knees, and legs—numbness, varicose veins, poor circulation, frostbite, knee or foot damage and pain, arthritic knees

Sapphire–Blue

Color: Blue
Chakra: Causal body

- Fills the hara line with light; increases communication with, connection to, and awareness of spirit guides, angels, the Light Body, oversoul, universal mind grid, and Goddess
- Activates and manifests one's life purpose and brings it into earthplane consciousness, focuses intent and awareness on fulfilling one's life purpose and karmic agreements for soul growth
- Brings gifts of fulfillment—joy, prosperity, inner peace, beauty—into one's life

This stone has powerful and transformative gemstone energy that may work quickly and drastically.

Sapphire–Star (natural only)

Color: Blue and silver
Chakra: Causal body

- Promotes connection with other-dimensional and other-planetary information for healing oneself and others
- Aids teachers of healing and healers in becoming clear channels for healing, facilitates connection and working with angelic Be-ings in healing
- Supports those in service to others and the planet; aids becoming an old soul, becoming a bodhisattva
- Eases healers' burnout, aids healers' own healing needs

Sapphire–Yellow

Color: Gold, yellow
Chakra: Hara chakra

- Moves life force energy through the hara line channels and the Ch'i Kung microcosmic orbit, expands the hara's ability to hold Earth and Heavenly Ch'i
- Increases spiritual energy through the etheric and emotional bodies
- Intensifies commitment to one's life purpose and karmic agreements, aids in fulfilling one's path
- Contributes to abundance and prosperity
- Heals burnout, depression, lack of energy, chronic fatigue

Sea Glass

Color: Clear, colors
Chakra: chakra matches color

- Promotes awareness of one's connection with all other people and Be-ings, promotes awareness that all life is one life
- Reinforces connection with the sea, sea creatures, ocean Goddesses; conducts messages from dolphins, whales, sea turtles; engenders awareness that all life comes from the sea
- Furthers water environmentalism, protecting the sea and sea life
- Invokes knowledge and fond memory of the womb, soothes and calms

*Selenite–Angel Wing
※

Color: White
Chakra: Transpersonal point

- Moves one's energy upwards on the hara line, fills the hara line with light
- Aids connection with and channeling of one's spirit guides, angels, and other discarnate helpers and healers
- Aids connection with angelic realms and positive other-planetary Be-ings
- Gives security and certainty of one's place in the universe, promotes knowledge of self as far more than this lifetime in the body
- Expands knowledge of soul structure and between-life states, soul and oversoul; repairs twelve strand DNA
- Contributes to core soul healing, heals and calms

This stone is very fragile.

Selenite–Clear
※

Color: Clear, white
Chakra: Transpersonal point

- Opens, aligns, and clears the aura bodies; opens energy blocks; fills the aura with light; transmits light/information/energy/ch'i; aids ascension
- Heals the Light Body, connects with the Earth and inter-planetary grids, repairs twelve-strand DNA
- Brings information from the Pleiades, gives protection, transforms and heals negativity, aids channeling

Selenite–Desert Rose

✦

Color: Beige, white
Chakra: Vision

- Produces spiritual nourishment, connects with the Mother Goddess
- Engenders the feeling of being cared for, being safe and cared about, and being taken care of by the universe and the Mother
- Brings about security, safety, the feeling that all is well; creates inner peace
- Aids in knowing that one is valued in the universal plan
- Helps nursing mothers to have enough breast milk, aids in giving nourishment as well as in receiving it

Selenite–Hour Glass

✦

Color: Clear, orange
Chakra: Hara chakra

- Fits one's life purpose into one's lifetime, promotes fulfillment of life goals for this incarnation
- Helps to complete and manifest one's life agreements and attain agreed-upon soul growth while there is time to do so
- Fosters awareness of time as a physical limit, stops procrastination
- Clears the hara and hara line channels

Selenite–Phantom

✦

Color: Clear and tan
Chakra: Movement

- Brings spiritual level knowledge into earthplane action, connects spirituality to daily life

- Fills the entire hara line/emotional body with light; clears, balances, and stabilizes all the hara chakras
- Aids neurological dis-eases, injuries, and traumas; heals strokes; aids insomnia; alleviates nightmares and night terrors
- Calms, balances, stabilizes, heals, and soothes

Septarian–Brown
※

Color: Brown and black
Chakra: Grounding

- Promotes the ability for a one-pointed earthplane focus, aids doing one thing at a time and completing it before going to something else
- Helps those who procrastinate, grounds scattered and diffused energy
- Aids moving forward on one's path in a self-directed and focused way, encourages certainty of one's path on the earthplane
- Calms, grounds, and centers

Septarian–Yellow
※

Color: Yellow and tan
Chakra: Solar plexus

- Opens the solar plexus for concentrated energy intake, assimilation, and one-pointed focus
- Takes in energy and psychic information from and about other people when they are focused upon (physically present or not), directs concentrated psychic focus
- Aids nonverbal and psychic communication between people, reduces distraction and scattering of mental energy

- Increases psychic impressions and information; helps psychic healers, psychic readers, tarot readers

Seraphanite
※

Color: Grey, silver
Chakra: Vision

- Aligns the soul bodies, opens and aligns the Body of Light to the astral body vibration
- Harmonizes energy vibration rates among the bodies and chakras, brings one's astral twin self into the physical level aura, purifies the aura
- Aids in contact with spirit guides, angels, and Goddess; brings awareness of one's place in the universal plan
- Supports psychic vision, enhances spiritualized seeing of the world
- Promotes peace in the world and in oneself

Serpentine
※

Color: Light green
Chakra: Diaphragm

- Clears, develops, and expands the hara line's ability to hold energy
- Detoxifies and clears the hara chakras and hara line of blockages
- Aids grounding and cleansing, moves energy in a strong downward stream that may not be comfortable

This stone is not a major healing energy.

Shiva Lingam

Color: brown and red
Chakra: Perineum

- Increases connection with of Shiva and Kali, the Goddess and the god *(Shiva is considered to be male but was originally female.)*
- Raises and grounds the kundalini, connects kundalini and hara lines, promotes grounding into one's incarnation and the body
- Facilitates the union of body and soul and the union of male and female
- Enhances sexuality, fosters sexual healing (especially for men), brings transformation

Lingams are generally seen as representing the penis, male sexuality, and the male god aspect.

Silver Aura Crystal

Color: Clear, iridescent
Chakra: Transpersonal point

- Fills the auric envelope with light at the etheric and astral body levels, heals the etheric and emotional body aura
- Repairs energy tears, protects the aura from others' negative energy and psychic attacks
- Clears negative energy from the aura (not the chakras)

Also see Aqua Aura Crystal.

Smithsonite–Aqua

Color: aqua
Chakra: Thymus

- Opens oneself to repressed emotions in order to clear and heal them; heals grief, rage, anger, resentment, sadness, sorrow, heartache
- Supports the release process and makes it gentle
- Heals the fear of one's own strong emotions, speeds the releasing
- Refills the aura with peace, healing, and security

Smithsonite–Pink

Color: Pink
Chakra: Heart

- Aids in trusting others and oneself, trusting in Goddess
- Opens one up to let others in, lets down walls that block one's heart growth and joy, opens the heart
- Helps one learn to love and give to others, releases resentment and blame, aids in forgiving others and oneself

Soapstone

Color: White
Chakra: Vision

- Aids visualization, promotes the ability to see the finished figure in the lump of stone
- Inspires creativity, sculpting

- Aids in creating a visualized reality, makes a dream come alive through artistry and expertise, guides artists to their highest potential
- Aids working with the hands and finishing the projects one begins

*Sodalite
---☼---

Color: Blue and white
Chakra: Third eye

- Balances the pituitary gland and third eye chakra; heals the lymphatic and glandular systems, nerve endings, vision nerves
- Encourages beginning psychic vision, helps new psychics to accept opening, calms fear of one's psychic vision and abilities
- Aids in letting go of control and trusting the Goddess and the process
- Soothes and heals the central nervous system

Sphalerite
---☼---

Color: Black
Chakra: Earth chakra

- Helps other-planetary souls now in Earth bodies to feel a part of life on this planet
- Helps one to feel like one belongs here, heals loneliness, decreases alienation from others and society, lessens feeling different and isolated
- Alleviates homesickness for one's star home
- Aids environmental illnesses, promotes grounding

Spinel–Red
※

Color: Red
Chakra: Perineum

- Aligns the etheric and emotional aura bodies, connects the kundalini and hara lines
- Rejuvenates, regenerates, detoxifies the etheric double aura
- Lengthens life by balancing ch'i energy and removing blocks to energy flow, brings Earth Ch'i into the body, stimulates the Ch'i Kung microcosmic orbit through the aura electrical system
- Acts as a gateway of life and death, incarnation and reincarnation
- Increases physical vitality, refills spent energy, aids exhaustion

Staurolite (Fairy Cross)
※

Color: Grey, black
Chakra: Vision

- Aids in seeing the world as the fairies and "little people" see it; helps one to see nature devas, Earth elementals, water spirits and tree spirits, and to work co-creatively with the unseen world
- Helps gardeners, flower essence therapists, crystal healers
- Enlists the help of Earth spirits and Mother Earth, heals with the aid of nature and the planet
- Honors the four directions, increases awareness of "as above so below"

Stilbite

Color: Orange and clear
Chakra: Hara chakra

- Connects the transpersonal point to the hara chakra, brings energy as information through the whole hara line
- Aids psychic knowing, guidance, and direction
- Brings information about the soul, soul structure, spiritual realities
- Fosters core soul healing and increases the ability to receive spiritual energy and psychic information
- Promotes access to the Living Library, increases reception of Heavenly Ch'i, clears and cleanses the hara chakra

*Sugilite

Color: Purple and black
Chakra: Crown

- Opens, clears, and balances the kundalini channels and kundalini chakras
- Helps the spiritual Be-ing to live well on the earthplane, cushions the Earth's harshness for spiritually oriented Be-ings
- Aids living in the present rather than dwelling on the past or future, transcends the limits of time
- Heals the body via the mind, promotes karmic healing and connection to the Nonvoid and Goddess within
- Tunes one's personal vibration to that of the Earth and planetary mind grids
- Releases and heals despair, releases hostility, eases discouragement
- Balances left and right hemispheres of the brain; aids dyslexia, strokes, epilepsy

Sulfur

Color: Yellow
Chakra: Diaphragm

- Detoxifies the physical body of dis-eases with emotional origins
- Heals karmic dis-eases by releasing their source in this life or in past lifetimes
- Focuses primarily on this life dis-eases manifested in the body from the past and carried over from other lifetimes
- Heals skin conditions, asthma, lung dis-eases

Sunstone–Orange

Color: Orange gold
Chakra: Hara chakra

- Clears blockages in the hara chakra, supports the life force and the hara line
- Clears impediments to fulfilling one's life purpose, helps in completing karmic contracts and manifesting one's life purpose on the earthplane
- Evokes courage, heals fear, offers a candle of hope in the darkness

Sunstone–Yellow

Color: Golden
Chakra: Solar plexus

- Aids worldly success, promotes courage in work or business, creates prosperity
- Aids in finding a job and achieving success in keeping it

- Promotes organizational ability, mental clarity, intellectual stimulation; fosters alertness, self-confidence, and intuition in business and finance
- Increases ability to receive ideas and energy, fosters the assimilation of ideas and energy

Tanzanite

Color: Blue-violet
Chakra: Causal body

- Opens the causal body chakra to make new spiritual awareness possible, cleanses the emotional body at the spiritual chakra levels
- Promotes an interest in metaphysics, spirituality, and psychic work
- Opens an awareness of the comparison between how one lives and how one could choose to live more consciously, opens consciousness and awareness
- Aids in making spirituality-influenced life choices

Tektite

Color: Black
Chakra: Earth chakra

- Expands, aligns, and clears all the kundalini chakras and the kundalini line; connects kundalini and hara lines
- Protects energy; aids in grounding into Earth reality; brings safety and security
- Evokes positive help from non-Earth sources, aids connection to Pleiadian healers and planetary protectors
- Makes one a channel for extraterrestrial help for the planet
- Protects the aura against negative alien interference, aids in removing negative energy implants

Thulite

Color: Red
Chakra: Root

- Moves Earth energy upward through the kundalini chakras, balances and clears the chakras
- Brings rootedness in a grounded personal reality, aids life purpose and steadiness
- Inspires humility and a balanced ego, enhances recognition of self as a part of all life
- Balances women's reproductive system, aids premenstrual syndrome and intestinal and bowel dis-eases

Tiger Eye–Golden

Color: Gold, brown
Chakra: Solar plexus

- Makes one invisible to negative energy sources, protects against psychic attack
- Clears negative energy from the solar plexus, returns negative energy to its sender
- Protects travelers and automobiles from accidents
- Aids in ability to discern evil, aids physical vision

Tiger Eye–Red

Color: Red, brown
Chakra: Perineum chakra

- Connects kundalini and hara lines at the root/perineum, aids in drawing Earth energy into the body and chakra system

- Starts the flow of the Ch'i Kung microcosmic orbit through the hara line
- Increases life force energy through the hara channels, raises the kundalini

Tiger Iron (Tiger Eye with Hematite)
☼

Color: Brown and black
Chakra: Earth chakra

- Grounds, reduces stress by decreasing sensitivity
- Protects in war and danger
- Shields and closes the solar plexus chakra by grounding its energy into the Earth
- Helps those too psychically sensitive to city noise and pollution and those who take on others' emotions in crowds

This is a good stone for men and those whose new psychic opening is still ungrounded and untrained. Use only when needed, not for all-the-time wear.

Topaz–Blue
☼

Color: Light blue
Chakra: Throat

- Aids in feeling one's anger and releasing it, brings realization of one's emotions and emotional pain
- Helps one learn one's true and real feelings and honor them, helps one let go of anger and resentment
- Promotes surrender to forgiveness of oneself and others, gives one's pain to the Goddess for healing

Topaz–Champagne

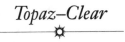

Color: Beige, tan
Chakra: Movement

- Brings spiritual level (hara line) energy into earthplane manifestation
- Increases energy movement from head to feet
- Causes life changes and transformations, transforms spiritual path inertia into Earth level physical movement
- Develops commitment to and fulfillment of karmic pre-life agreements and one's life purpose
- Ends procrastination when facing action and change, holds one to one's life path

Topaz–Clear

Color: Clear
Chakra: Transpersonal point

- Brings the energy of life change and transformation into the emotional body
- Initiates a time of change and transition, encourages positive breakthroughs
- Fosters growth, karmic clearing, core soul healing
- Induces sudden shifts in energy balance, releases negative entities and attachments

*Topaz–Golden

Color: Yellow
Chakra: Solar plexus

- Stabilizes life changes and transitions from birth to death, heals the etheric double aura

- Balances energy flows through the central nervous system
- Balances the alignment of body, mind, and emotions on all levels
- Clears and heals the Light Body, promotes reincarnation while in the body (total karmic life change)
- Stabilizes deep healing work and aura change, protects the aura during changes
- Releases and detoxifies, supports and heals the sacral-cranial spinal rhythm

*Tourmaline–Black

Color: Black
Chakra: Earth chakra

- Protects the aura and the incarnation, brings Earth energy into the root chakra and kundalini channels
- Acts as a protective shield, absorbs and transmutes negative energy and negative thought forms from oneself and others, offers protection from psychic attacks and spirit possessions
- Heals fear and panic, brings a sense of safety and security
- Activates the ability to ground and center, encourages rootedness into the Earth and the body
- Creates a feeling of being welcome on the earthplane, enhances the ability to stay in the body

Tourmaline–Black Velvet

Color: Black
Chakra: Earth chakra

- Opens and balances the hara line and all the hara chakras
- Brings a vibrating energy that expands, aligns, and opens energy blocks

- Heals obstructions that keep one's life purpose from being manifested, roots the incarnation's life agreements into physical achievement
- Aids connection to Earth Ch'i for nurturance from the planet
- Brings about entrance to the Void and Nonvoid for releasing limitations and negative karma
- Grounds and centers, enhances security, and stability

Tourmaline–Blue
❖

Color: Blue, blue-green
Chakra: Thymus

- Opens and clears the thymus chakra, connecting the hara line/emotional body to kundalini/etheric body channels
- Cleanses and stabilizes the hara line and hara chakras
- Transforms emotional healing into physical healing of dis-ease
- Focuses one's life purpose on service to the planet and people, fosters desire and dedication to one's life path and purpose, protects the full aura and one's life purpose
- Aids those who give too much in being able to receive, aids living the Bodhisattva Vow in balance
- Aids healers, promotes energy flow through the central nervous system

Tourmaline–Clear
❖

Color: Clear, silver
Chakra: Transpersonal point

- Offers all-aura protection, all-aura clearing
- Induces contact with positive extraterrestrial Be-ings, spirit guides, angels, ascended healers
- Aids channeling, automatic writing

- Clears and energizes the hara and kundalini channels, repairs twelve-strand DNA, heals core soul damage
- Aids in attaining karmic grace, fills all levels with information/light, is all-healing

*Tourmaline–Green
———————✸———————

Color: Green
Chakra: Diaphragm

- Opens and drains the diaphragm chakra, purges and releases negative emotions from the hara line and one's life purpose
- Clears the emotional body of past-life and this-life traumas and negative emotional patterns
- Protects while one is going through the detoxification process; offers aura insulation, safety, and trust while detoxifying; detoxifies the aura and chakras at etheric/kundalini and emotional/hara levels
- Clears the gall bladder and liver at the emotional level

The stone is deep-acting and fast-acting and can cause intense releases.

Tourmaline–Pink (Rubellite)
———————✸———————

Color: Red violet
Chakra: Causal body

- Brings deeply comforting love energy, opens and heals the entire emotional body
- Brings one's life purpose into all the hara chakras and into earthplane conscious awareness
- Balances energy flow in the hara and kundalini channels and chakras
- Removes blockages and negativity from the whole aura and chakra system at all levels

- Transforms negativity into positive emotional energy; fills emotional body and etheric body channels and chakras with light/information, peace, joy, universal love
- Promotes compassion for oneself and others and promotes a lifetime of service, supports those on the bodhisattva path

Tourmaline–Violet
☼

Color: Purple
Chakra: Crown

- Protects against, prevents, and clears spirit attachments, negative entities, spirit possession, and low-level entities
- Protects and releases negative alien implants and interference
- Clears the human energy system at etheric, emotional, mental, and light body levels of negative violations from this life only (will not heal those brought in from past lifetimes)
- Fills the kundalini and hara channels and aura bodies with light

Tourmaline–Watermelon
☼

Color: Pink and green
Chakra: Heart and causal body

- Heals and opens one's ability to reach out to others
- Fosters trust of self, others, and the Goddess; enhances self-love and universal love
- Encourages service to the planet, helps wounded healers and those who have suffered past abuse
- Heals and removes heart scars
- Brings one's pre-life karmic agreements and life purpose into one's heart, opens the heart and the causal body chakra

*Turquoise

Color: Aqua
Chakra: Thymus chakra

- Opens, clears, and develops the thymus chakra; connects the kundalini and hara line channels
- Heals this-life and past-life blocks in the throat chakra; opens, heals, and releases this-life and past-life fear and grief
- Heals sadness about one's life and deeds, heals karmic and this-life shame and guilt
- Connects physical and spiritual awareness, develops inner strength and calm
- Heals the emotions and emotional body, enhances communication and creativity

Ulexite (TV Stone)

Color: Clear
Chakra: Vision

- Inspires and stimulates visual imagery, brings visions and information from other dimensions and planets
- Provides a window on new and other worlds
- Promotes the ability to create and heal by visualization
- Aids willed transformations of reality, creates new opportunities and realities by allowing one to see them and then make them real
- Aids manifesting and brings precision in manifesting

Unakite

Color: Pink and green
Chakra: Diaphragm

- Clears the diaphragm chakra of toxic emotions and old pain
- Releases anger, resentment, and vengeance to conscious awareness for clearing
- Makes negative emotions abhorrent, forces transformation of negativity through awareness
- Fosters realization of the oneness of all life

Vanadinite

Color: Orange
Chakra: Belly

- Balances and shrinks uterine growths; heals endometriosis, uterine fibroid and other tumors
- Balances women's reproductive hormones, helps complete uterine lining clearing in menstruation
- Balances menopause symptoms, regulates menstrual cycles, aids premenstrual syndrome, brings on menses

Variscite

Color: Lime green
Chakra: Diaphragm

- Acts as a mild detoxifier of negative energy
- Stabilizes emotional release and healing from the diaphragm chakra
- Eases nausea and overwhelm from heavy detoxification and energy release

- Stabilizes the hara line after major healing work
- Helps to clear anesthetics and drugs from the body, alleviates postoperative nausea, helps to repair aura tears after anesthetics and surgeries

Wavellite

Color: Light green
Chakra: Diaphragm

- Prepares the diaphragm chakra for opening and clearing the emotional body
- Promotes readiness to heal emotional issues from this life and past lives
- Strengthens one emotionally to be able to heal and change
- Strengthens the diaphragm chakra's functioning ability to initiate and complete a detoxification process
- Aids emotional clearing at core soul levels

Wonderstone

Color: Orange, tan, colors
Chakra: Belly

- Aids in finding the positive pictures and images stored in the belly chakra, heals the wounded inner child
- Promotes appreciation of the diversity and wonder of life on Earth and one's own life in a body
- Allows one to see the benefits, positivity, or learning in any situation

• Stimulates curiosity, invokes the world through child's eyes

Most belly chakra gemstones release stored negative images for clearing; this one opens and reinforces good memories and the positive.

Wulfenite
☼

Color: Orange
Chakra: Belly

• Warms and energy-cleanses the inside of the uterus, promotes hormonal balance
• Brings on menstruation and promotes flow and full emptying of the uterus
• Clears the uterus after abortion, miscarriage, or childbirth
• Stabilizes sexual energy and sexuality
• Brings order out of confusion in relationships

Zincite–Crystalline
☼

Color: Red and gold
Chakra: Hara chakra

• Causes transformation in the fires of change for spiritual and karmic growth
• Refines dross into gold through wisdom
• Aids in fulfilling karmic agreements and one's life purpose
• Spurs reincarnation in this lifetime, aids walk-ins
• Brings spiritual purification; cleanses and clears the hara chakras and hara line/emotional body, stimulates energy

Zircon–Clear

Color: clear
Chakra: Transpersonal point

- Holds all the colors of the rainbow for appreciation of all peoples and cultures, reminds of the oneness of all life
- Aids in overcoming racism and ethnocentrism, in becoming a global citizen, and in overcoming the damage done to one's emotional body from being discriminated against through racism, ablism, homophobia, misogyny
- Heals victimization, promotes positive self-love, brings about love for others and respect for all

Full Moon in Cancer
January 5, 1996

Bibliography

Brennan, Barbara Ann. *Light Emerging: The Journey of Personal Healing.* New York: Bantam Books, 1993.

Brennan, Barbara Ann. *Hands of Light: A Guide to Healing through the Human Energy Field.* New York: Bantam Books, 1987.

Levine, Stephen. *Healing into Life and Death.* New York: Anchor Books, 1987.

Marciniak, Barbara. *Earth: Pleiadian Keys to the Living Library.* Santa Fe, N.M.: Bear & Co., 1995.

Marciniak, Barbara, and Tera Thomas, eds. *Bringers of the Dawn: Teachings from the Pleiadians.* Santa Fe, N.M.: Bear & Co., 1992.

Shealy, C. Norman, and Carolyn M. Myss *The Creation of Health: The Emotional, Psychological, and Spiritual Responses That Promote Health and Healing.*Walpole, N.H.: Stillpoint Publishing, 1993.

OTHER BOOKS BY DIANE STEIN

Psychic Healing with Spirit Guides and Angels

This book presents a complete program of soul development for self-healing, healing with others, and Earth healing. Many of the methods included in this book have never before been published. Advanced skills include healing karma and past lives, soul retrieval, releasing entities and spirit attachments, and understanding and aiding the death process.
$18.95 • Paper • 0-89594-807-9

Essential Reiki: A Complete Guide to an Ancient Healing Art

While no book can replace the directly received Reiki attunements, *Essential Reiki* provides everything else that the healer, practitioner, and the teacher of this system needs, including full information on all three degrees of Reiki, most of it in print for the first time.
$18.95 • Paper • 0-89594-736-6

The Natural Remedy Book for Women

This best-seller includes information on ten natural healing methods—vitamins and minerals, herbs, naturopathy, homeopathy and cell salts, amino acids, acupressure, aromatherapy, flower essences, gemstones and emotional healing. Remedies from all ten methods are given for fifty common health problems.
$16.95 • Paper • 0-89594-525-8

Grief and Dying: Understanding the Soul's Journey

Guiding the reader on a healing journey to a place of loving acceptance, this book offers comfort and help to persons facing death and to those who love them.
$15.00 • Hardcover • ISBN 0-89594-830-3

OTHER BOOKS BY DIANE STEIN

*All Women Are Healers: A Comprehensive Guide
to Natural Healing*
A wealth of "how-to" information on various healing methods including Reiki, reflexology, polarity balancing, and
homeopathy, intended to teach women to take control of
their bodies and lives.
$14.95 · Paper · 0-89594-409-X

Natural Healing for Dogs & Cats
Tells how to use nutrition, vitamins, minerals, massage, herbs,
homeopathy, acupuncture, acupressure, and flower essences,
as well as owner-pet communication and psychic healing.
$16.95 • Paper • ISBN 0-89594-614-9

The Natural Remedy Book for Dogs & Cats
The perfect companion to Stein's earlier book- Natural
Healing for Dogs and Cats. Fifty common pet ailments and
remedies are arranged in alphabetical order. Methods of
treatment including nutrition, naturopathy, vitamins and
minerals, herbs, homeopathy, acupuncture/acupressure,
flower essences, and gemstones are discussed for each illness.
$16.95 • Paper • ISBN 0-89594-686-6

Casting the Circle: A Women's Book of Ritual
$14.95 • Paper • 0-89594-411-1

*The Goddess Celebrates: An Anthology
of Women's Rituals*
Contributors include Z. Budapest, Starhawk, and others.
$14.95 • Paper • 0-89594-460-X